Biodiversity for
Low and Zero Carbon Buildings

Biodiversity for Low and Zero Carbon Buildings

A Technical Guide for New Build

Dr Carol Williams

of the Bat Conservation Trust

RIBA Publishing

© Dr Carol Williams, 2010

Published by RIBA Publishing, 15 Bonhill Street, London EC2P 2EA

ISBN 978 1 85946 353 6

Stock code 70194

The right of Dr Carol Williams to be identified as the Author of this Work has been asserted in accordance with the Copyright, Design and Patents Act 1988.

British Library Cataloguing in Publications Data
A catalogue record for this book is available from the British Library.

Publisher: Steven Cross
Commissioning Editor: Lucy Harbor
Project Editor: Alex Lazarou
Designed and typeset by Alex Lazarou
Printed and bound by Polestar Wheatons

While every effort has been made to check the accuracy and quality of the information given in this publication, neither the Author nor the Publisher accept any responsibility for the subsequent use of this information, for any errors or omissions that it may contain, or for any misunderstandings arising from it.

RIBA Publishing is part of RIBA Enterprises Ltd.
www.ribaenterprises.com

contents

foreword

Swifts screaming round the rooftops must be one of the most evocative sounds of summer. Sadly, these great travellers have been in steady decline, with numbers down by 29% between 1995 and 2007. The reasons for this decline may be complex, but one way we can help is to make sure that a shortage of good nesting sites is not part of the problem.

As we move towards a low carbon economy, reducing the energy we use to heat our homes has surely got to be one of the quickest wins, so Natural England is firmly behind the move towards zero and low energy building policies. At the same time, we believe it is important that the emerging standards for sustainable development, such as the Code for Sustainable Homes, pay more than lip-service to addressing the ecological impacts of development and make a real contribution to biodiversity.

The adoption of new construction techniques, with much more focus on structural integrity, carries with it a real threat to the many species of birds and bats (in particular) that have been able to exploit opportunities left by traditional building practices and imperfect workmanship. Many of these species now rely heavily on buildings and some, such as the Serotine bat, are rarely found roosting elsewhere. Many depend on particular features of buildings that are likely to be lost with new construction techniques, for example swifts will be denied the holes and crevices they need and bats will no longer be able to find their way into roof voids.

If we are not to see a slow decline in the resources available to these animals, we need to act now to combat this loss of residential opportunities. In particular, we need to be much more proactive in providing tailor-made opportunities, rather than leaving it to chance and poor workmanship. This groundbreaking book brings together information about the needs of wildlife and the details of new building techniques to show how such opportunities can be built in at virtually no cost and with no adverse effect on the performance of the building. We now look to the architectural community to use these ideas imaginatively to ensure that every new development offers wildlife opportunities within the buildings. This will complement the work we all need to do to make space for wildlife in the surrounding green infrastructure.

Helen Phillips
Chief Executive
Natural England

acknowledgements

Nine months after we first conceived the idea for this book, we will be attending the launch at EcoBuild 2010. Anyone who has published a book will tell you that the author, Dr Carol Williams, must be to publishing what Usain Bolt is to sprinting. This would not have been possible without the immense amount of effort that Carol has put into the research and the writing of this book, and she has been supported by her employer, the Bat Conservation Trust, who recognised the value in producing this much-needed guidance and allowed her to spend staff time working on this book.

The Bat Conservation Trust is the only national organisation solely devoted to the conservation of bats and their habitats in the UK and is working towards a world where bats and people thrive together.

I would like to thank Natural England who have generously provided funding to commission the architectural research and drawings for the book. Natural England works for people, places and nature to conserve and enhance biodiversity, landscapes and wildlife in rural, urban, coastal and marine areas. They conserve and enhance the natural environment for its intrinsic value, the well-being and enjoyment of people and the economic prosperity it brings.

I would also like to thank the Barn Owl Trust, GreenSpec and Swift Conservation who have all been valuable contributors to the book.

Lucy Harbor
Commissioning Editor
RIBA Publishing

preface

In March 2009, the UK Green Building Council Biodiversity Task Group launched its report and associated recommendations. The Group was established in June 2008 and brought together a cross section of the construction industry and experts on biodiversity to undergo an intense period of focus on the range of issues that act as barriers that prevent the incorporation of biodiversity into sustainable construction.

As part of this wide-ranging endeavour, a review was undertaken by the Group of all the information available on biodiversity and the built environment, including reports, documents and websites. Among their findings, the Group recognised that some gaps in available information exist, particularly in relation to making provision for species when designing new low or zero carbon buildings.

This book aims to bridge that identified gap in knowledge by providing factual and practical advice on how to make new buildings truly sustainable.

By recognising the need for new low and zero carbon buildings which comply with the stringent requirements of future house building – in terms of the carbon footprint and, at the same time, which deliver a biodiversity gain for protected species – the book describes how to build genuinely sustainable buildings.

A brief overview is given of wildlife and planning legislation, the Biodiversity Action Planning Process and the building regulations which relate to low and zero carbon buildings. It indicates where it is possible to find out more on these specialist areas, about which an extensive range of publications and websites is available.

This book is not about mitigation for existing roosts and nesting places. It is not intended to take the place of an environmental ecologist and it is expected that the choice of provision for enhancing biodiversity of the built structures, as well as advice on how that provision can be accommodated within any development, will be guided by an experienced ecologist.

It is also important to emphasise that the book is about enhancement for biodiversity in new build and is not about refurbishment to existing housing stock. I am often asked about enhancement for biodiversity during refurbishment – increasingly retrofitting to reduce energy wastage. This is a whole different subject and one for which some existing publications will prove helpful and for which some principles in this book would apply. Of course, where protected species are already present, the existing system of advice or licensing will operate. However, the retrofitting of energy saving measures is a quickly developing part of the industry, and brings new opportunities and challenges for enhancement for building-reliant biodiversity. As the potential for existing housing stock is so vast, this is a subject that needs serious consideration and collaborative working in order to reach solutions, and may be considered for a separate publication.

It is such collaborative working that has brought about this publication. Without the close working between conservation organisations and professionals from the construction industry, this book would never have come into being. In particular, I would like to thank the architects who have been so fundamental to the practical advancement made: the drawings from Will Paul and Kirkland Fraser Moor architects; and also the development of these drawings and advice on all aspects of the book and sustainable building from Brian Murphy of GreenSpec. His drive and enthusiasm gave more than was ever anticipated. I must also acknowledge the vital input from my colleagues, in particular the funding that has enabled this book to come to fruition – thank you to Natural England, who not only gave financial support, but also support in a much wider sense through Tony Mitchell-Jones and Allan Drewitt. Important input was also made freely available by David Ramsden and Matthew Twiggs of the Barn Owl Trust, and by Edward Mayer of Swift Conservation. To all the staff at the Bat Conservation Trust, I would like to offer my gratitude for their assistance in sharing my workload so that I could dedicate my time to this book. In particular, Sarah Ford for being my proof-reader and for doing so much more.

Finally, I would like to thank all of the following who were kind enough to review this book and offer constructive and astute observations: Tony Mitchell-Jones, Allan Drewitt, Brian Murphy, Mike Oxford, John Newman, Ellie Austin, Paul King, Edward Mayer, Shirley Thompson, Richard Crompton and Professor Paul Racey.

The information contained within this book may prove to be less than perfect, which is wholly my responsibility, and in the future I may look back and blush. But, it is, I hope, a valuable contribution to truly sustainable building and will lead the way to future collaborative working between these two sectors, making the best use of the knowledge in our possession.

Carol Williams
Bat Conservation Trust

introduction

When sustainable building is being considered, there has been a tendency to focus on carbon- and material-related issues, while biodiversity has been given limited consideration. The definition of sustainable building that was provided by the Department for Trade and Industry* lists the need to preserve and enhance biodiversity, alongside energy and waste considerations, and for very good reason. Biodiversity is not an additional option in an ideal world, but a fundamental need – not only in the context of truly sustainable building, but also for our quality of life and the long-term sustainability of our planet. This integral role of biodiversity in sustainable construction has been consolidated by the inclusion of a chapter on the subject in the *Strategy for Sustainable Construction*, published in 2008 by BERR on behalf of the Government and the construction industry.

But what do we mean when we say that biodiversity is a fundamental need? Taking the wider view, biological diversity (biodiversity) of wildlife, plants and their habitats is a vital component of healthy, well-functioning ecosystems, which, in turn, sustain all life on the planet. This can be in the form of our food; either directly or via the reliance on pollinators, seed dispersers, or the web of organisms and habitats that relate to aspects of our diet. Our health is linked to biodiversity in several ways; for example, some new drugs and treatments are developed from the natural world around us, and access to nature helps both our physical and mental health. Horwitz *et al.* (2001) found that native biodiversity can contribute to a sense of place and belonging, and a lack of biodiversity may, therefore, negatively affect both well-being and community identity. Of course, there are also direct resources from nature, such as timber, and a host of natural fibres and fuels.

'Ecosystem services' is a term widely used when talking about the value of nature and biodiversity. Basically, it refers to natural processes such as those that clean our air and water, provide protection to our coasts from erosion, and provide defence against flooding and soil erosion. The need for these services grows ever greater as we enter a period of uncertainty and a shift in climatic patterns, leading to more stochastic weather patterns as a result of climate change. Recent research from the European Commission highlights how 'the well-being of every human population in the world is fundamentally and directly dependent on ecosystem services' (EC, 2008). For a comprehensive account of ecosystem services, see *The Economics of Ecosystems and Biodiversity* (EC, 2008).

This is a global outlook, but what is the state of biodiversity in the UK and how much do we value it? A report by Natural England (2009) shows how the economic value of nature now runs to billions of pounds in the UK alone. But the picture is one that gives cause for some concern:

- 39% of habitats and 27% of 'priority species' are in decline, with some showing accelerated deterioration (Defra, 2006);
- bird numbers have been depleted by an average of 6% in the last 30 years (Defra, 2008a);
- butterfly populations have dropped an average of 55% in the last 30 years (Defra, 2008b); and
- major declines in bees, arable plants and amphibians have also been recorded (Margerison, 2008).

* The Department for Trade and Industry was replaced in 2007 by the Department for Business, Enterprise and Regulatory Reform (BERR) and the Department for Innovation, Universities and Skills (DIUS). On 6 June 2009 BERR itself was disbanded following the creation of the Department for Business, Innovation and Skills (BIS).

Our built environment has the potential to have major negative impacts on biodiversity. However, if done sensitively, the development and refurbishment of buildings can, in fact, increase the ecological value of the site.

There is a growing body of research that suggests that access to biodiversity and green spaces is valuable to individuals, businesses and communities. Research by the Commission for Architecture and the Built Environment (CABE) concludes that property values increase near green spaces, with houses close to parks averaging 8% higher prices than similar properties further away (CABE, 2005a). A report by Natural Economy Northwest (NEN) found that businesses located in greener settings attract and retain more motivated staff, and that green spaces near work places lead to reduced sickness and increased productivity (NEN, 2008). A Government led project is underway on the subject of the 'Economic Valuation of the Benefits of the UK Biodiversity Action Plan'. This is a piece of research seeking to quantify and value the benefits of achieving the UK biodiversity targets.

Bird species and, more recently, bats have been recognised as indicators of biodiversity by the Government and as such are used as a sign of the general state of biodiversity in the UK. With a number of bat and bird species relying on built structures, the impact of the building and construction industry can be significant.

Despite this, the information that is available is largely concerned with situations where the wildlife has become established in existing buildings and not when new buildings are being planned or designed. In new developments the potential for biodiversity in the built structures themselves has been given virtually no consideration at all. The likely reason for this is that traditional building styles have always been such that the wildlife that has become associated with our buildings over many centuries has continued to find its niche.

However, the very real need for low or zero carbon buildings has led to new building techniques, materials and designs being developed. The one thing that all of these innovative advances have in common is the need for an 'airtight' barrier that encompasses the utilised part of the building. The result of this is that, while striving to reduce the carbon footprint of our buildings, for the first time since humans made shelters for themselves, the species that share these buildings with us, such as swifts, swallows and bats, will no longer find a potential resting, nesting or roosting place.

In addition, the National Standard *Building for Life* has a criterion that the 'internal spaces and layout allow for adaptation, conversion or extension' which is likely to lead to most new dwellings having the U value envelope reaching up to the apex of the roof to allow for future conversions of the roof space into a living area.

The wildlife that has historically shared our built structures includes some of the most valued and vulnerable in Britain; whether it is our migratory birds that fly thousands of miles across hazardous terrain to reach our shores; or our own populations of sparrows and starlings, now in sharp decline; or the enigmatic barn owl, swooping majestically and silently through the adjacent countryside. Bats are so important in our ecosystems that they are now recognised by the Government as indicators of biodiversity and yet their numbers have plummeted.

So is the situation hopeless? Does the need to reduce the carbon footprint of buildings mean that these species, that are a vital part of our ecosystem, that keep that important balance in nature and that give joy to so many, are destined to suffer even greater threats as new buildings become barren deserts to them? Thankfully, the answer is no. It is entirely possible to continue to see these building-reliant species thrive in low and zero carbon buildings, but the difference is we need to consider biodiversity early on in the design process and to incorporate measures, which generally incur little extra expense, into buildings.

This book takes what we know of the needs of our building-reliant species and, at the same time, reviews the build types that are likely to be in general use over the next decade. With due consideration for the Building Regulations, a series of architect's drawings are presented that are suitable for the enhancement of biodiversity in new low or zero carbon buildings.

As well as helping to maintain and enhance the populations of these species, there can actually be benefits to incorporating these bespoke roosting and nesting places. In traditional styles of building, the bats and birds could utilise any number of opportunities within a building. Sometimes this could lead to conflict with the human residents, or could conflict with other uses or future plans for the building. The need for bespoke roosting and nesting places means that the species in question will be contained in those areas so conflicts with the human residents can be avoided in the vast majority of cases.

Although this book concentrates on this important subject area – for which no guidance previously exists – it is recognised that buildings are an opportunity for a greater range of wildlife than just birds and bats. Living roofs and walls are becoming ever more popular and with very good reason. Standard roofs (non-living) cover a huge area and, for the most part, are without merit either to look at or for biodiversity. A living roof is not only visually appealing, but is good for wildlife, important in reducing the likelihood of flood events (by retaining rainwater to later evaporate and also by modifying the effects of rainfall), and as a buffer for the building against extremes of temperature.

It is acknowledged that the inclusion of roosting and nesting potential in low and zero carbon buildings is an evolving practice. Therefore, while the designs given are informed by best current knowledge, it is vital that the uptake of these opportunities is monitored. It is only by this sort of feedback that we can learn the relative success of designs and products, and adjust future advice on provision accordingly. The expected delay in uptake by some species will be taken into account during this process.

In the future, it would be a positive step indeed if we could see our new built environments reflecting the rich wildlife heritage that we have inherited in the UK.

chapter one

Biodiversity and the importance of buildings

1.1 About bats and buildings

1.1.1 Bats worldwide

There are over 1,100 species of bats worldwide, and they account for a fifth of all mammals. Bats can be as small as a bumble bee or as large as a small dog. On a global scale, bats are one of the most widely distributed groups of mammals and are found across every land mass, apart from the Arctic, the Antarctic and a few isolated oceanic islands. There are bats in the far north of Scandinavia, as well as in the deserts of south-west USA.

Bats are most numerous in the tropics. Most bats eat insects, but some feed on pollen and nectar, while others eat fruit. A few highly specialised bats feed on fish, frogs and even on other bats. There are also the three species of vampire bats, which feed on blood, that are found only in central and South America.

Approximately 25% of the world's bats are threatened with extinction.

1.1.2 Bats in the UK

There are 17 species of bat native to the UK. They are all small and there are a number of aspects of their ecology that they all have in common. They are all nocturnal and eat insects. Although all the UK bats have reasonable eyesight, when flying and looking for insect prey in darkness it is their ears that are more important than their eyes. This is because they use echolocation, which is a system of shouting at a high pitch (above our hearing range) and listening for the returning echoes. This gives the bats a very clear picture of their surroundings and also of the location and direction of the movement of insects.

The insects on which British bats feed cover a wide range, dependent on the size of the bat species and the habitats over which they feed. The UK bat species all tend to favour different methods of hunting and have different habitats that they favour. The larger UK bats can feed on beetles as big as May bugs and dung beetles, while the smaller bats feed on smaller insects, such as gnats, crane flies and midges, up to 3,000 of which can be consumed by a bat in one night. Unsurprisingly, bats are most likely to be found feeding over habitats that support an abundance of insects, such as water, native woodland, hedgerows, unimproved meadows and grassland, mature gardens and grazed pasture where dung fauna are important. Table 1.1 gives a summary of the annual cycle of UK bats.

Table 1.1: Annual cycle of UK bats

Season	Activity
Autumn	The young born during summer are feeding independently
	All bats are feeding to put on weight for the winter
	Mating begins
Winter	Hibernation (consisting of prolonged bouts of torpor)
	Bats (particularly smaller species) feed during mild spells
Spring	Hibernation ends and females become pregnant
	In late spring females gather in maternity roosts which need to be warm
	Non-breeding adults are found as individuals or in small numbers in cooler roosts
Summer	The single young is born and is suckled by the mother for four to five weeks

The roosts used by bats are often the same ones that have been used year after year for generations. Bats are long lived, with even the smallest of the UK bat species likely to live into their teens and larger UK bats have been recorded living into their thirties in the wild. However, having only one young per year means that bat populations are very slow to recover from changes to the environment, such as the loss of prey species or the loss of roosts, which threaten their ability to survive or breed.

All the UK bat populations declined considerably during the last century, although a number of species have, in recent years, shown some signs of recovery. The declines were largely due to human factors – such as the loss of feeding habitats, the use of pesticides and intensive farming practices reducing the abundance of insects, and building and development work affecting roosts – and these declines are the reason that all UK bats and their roosts are now protected by law (see Chapter 2).

1.1.3 Importance of buildings for bats

All British bat species will make some use of buildings, but, for many species, buildings are essential as roost sites. This situation has arisen over a long period of time as trees and the availability of caves, which would have provided their natural roost sites, have become scarce. Hundreds of years ago bat species began to share our built structures with us.

For several weeks in the summer, female bats choose somewhere warm to gather in a maternity roost, such as a roof area heated by the sun or in features in a wall that is south facing. At the same time, non-breeding adults find cooler roosts, such as north-facing features, where bats are found in small numbers or singly.

Bats can be found roosting in both old and new buildings, although a greater number of roosts and range of species are found in older buildings. The type of places bats use to roost might be within the roof void or within a cavity wall, but some species will tend to use external features, such as hanging tiles, weather boarding, fascias, soffits and barge boards. Bats do not take any material into the roost with them, nor do they chew wires.

Common pipistrelle in
woodcrete box

When considering the roosting habits of bats in buildings, it is useful to
make an arbitrary division between those crevice-dwelling species that roost
in external features or that only require a small crevice type of provision
within the structure and those bats that require flying space within the
building. A further distinction is needed within this group of bats that
require flight space, and that concerns access to the roost, since horseshoe
bats have different needs to all other UK bat species.

The greater and lesser horseshoe bats are the only two species of bat in
the UK that have adapted to hanging free by their feet when roosting.
These are two of our rarest bat species, with a very close association with
buildings and are among those which have suffered the steepest decline in
numbers, although both species are showing signs of reversing that trend
in recent years. Their range within the UK has also become reduced and
they are now only found in Wales and South West England. Horseshoe bats'
adaptation to hanging free by their feet has resulted in a specialisation of
their leg structure, which means that they are unable to crawl effectively –
unlike all other UK species of bat. The consequence is that, where other bat

Brown long-eared bats

Greater horseshoe bats

species can access their roost though a small gap, horseshoe bats need to fly into their roosts. This requirement has threatened their survival, as many large manor houses, barns and other outbuildings were converted and the access points used by bats lost prior to the time when bats were legally protected (1981).

Table 1.2 lists the categories within which the UK bat species fall, but it is important to note that this is only an arbitrary grouping and the type of roost (maternity, non-breeding adults, transitory, mating, hibernaculum, night or feeding roosts), or the part of the country they are located in, will all make a difference to what bats require of a roost. To describe these finer details of bat roosting ecology is beyond the scope of this book. An experienced bat ecologist should be consulted over this level of detail.

Roosts in existing building stock are vitally important and a future book is being considered that will look at the issues surrounding the refurbishment and retrofitting of our current housing stock to achieve low carbon buildings. But this book is concerned with looking to the future and the requirement for low and zero carbon homes, and incorporating provision for bats as enhancement. In more traditional designs, some potential for crevice-dwelling bat species may remain also where weather boarding/ wood cladding is used. However, without positive, proactive measures, the fact is that future housing stock will, in general, contain no potential roosts for the majority of bat species.

Table 1.2: The roosting preferences of UK bat species

Category	Bat species
Crevice-dwelling bats (that tend to be hidden from view) and	Common pipistrelle, soprano pipistrelle, Nathusius' pipistrelle, Brandt's, whiskered
roof-void dwelling bats (that may be visible on roof timbers)	Noctule, serotine, Leisler's, Daubenton's, greater mouse-eared, barbastelle and Bechstein's
Bats that need flight space in certain types of roost	Natterer's, and brown and grey long-eared
Bats that need flight space and flying access	Greater horseshoe, lesser horseshoe

1.2 About birds and buildings

There are a number of bird species for whom buildings are important. This book concentrates on those with the strongest association and reliance on buildings. But there are other birds, such as the pied wagtail, wren, little owl and black redstart, that are also known to utilise buildings. Many of the measures discussed in this book will also offer opportunities for use by these species.

There are those species that have travelled a great many miles to spend the summer months in the UK where they rear their young. It is these birds – the swallow, house martin and swift – that we will consider first.

1.2.1 Swifts

While the swift (*Apus apus*) has a physical appearance that is similar to the other two migratory species mentioned in this book (the swallow and house martin), it actually belongs to a separate family that has evolved to utilise insect prey in the same way. Swifts are particularly remarkable for their feat of staying on the wing. A young swift will spend its first two or three years in constant flight before it breeds. Swifts sleep and mate on the wing.

Swifts breed throughout Europe and as far north as Lapland and the Arctic Circle, reaching east across Asia to China. They are in the UK for only a short period of time compared with most other summer migrants. They arrive in the last week of April or early May and, having bred, begin their return migration in late July or early August. Our UK swifts migrate to Africa to spend their winter south of the Equator.

Swift

Swifts traditionally nested in crags, sea cliffs, caves, hollow trees and nest holes made by other birds. These sites have been almost entirely replaced by nesting in buildings, upon which the species has become reliant right across Europe and parts of Asia. In the UK these amazing birds have shared our buildings ever since the Romans came to Britain. However, this could come to an end with the introduction of low and zero carbon structures unless we make specific provision for swifts when designing buildings.

A typical swift's nest is located high up in man-made structures, traditionally under tiles, in the eaves, behind gables, and in the lofts, spires and towers of old houses and other structures, such as churches or industrial buildings. The height (in excess of 3 m) of the nest from the ground is important, as swifts swoop in and out of the nest entrance at high speed to avoid predation. The nest is built by both adults out of any wind-borne material that can be gathered on the wing, including feathers, leaves, paper, straw and man-made materials. The nest is cemented together with their saliva, and is renovated and reused year after year, as swifts pair for life. But the pairs are not usually solitary; breeding is stimulated by the presence of other pairs nearby and swifts indulge in much colonial aerial activity, notably their spectacular screaming flights. Swifts can thrive right in the heart of major towns and cities, provided the nest places are there for them.

Swifts do a lot of good, do no harm and make little or no mess. As the parent birds remove most of the chicks' droppings, there are rarely many droppings beneath their nests. Swifts eat only flying insects, including a huge number of aphids, gnats and mosquitoes, catching thousands each and every day, and so bringing significant benefits in the control of harmful insects.

On summer evenings and early in the mornings, you might see excited screaming parties of swifts careering madly at high speed around rooftops, often flying low. It is a sound of summer, even for the most urban environments. However, the UK swift population, estimated at 80,000 birds in 1990, has since decreased by as much as 50%. If we want to keep this spectacular and beneficial visitor for generations to come, we need to make proper provision for them now.

1.2.2 Swallows

The swallow (*Hirundo rustica*) is probably our most famous summer visitor. Well distributed throughout Britain and Ireland, it arrives in the UK around mid-April, having flown 10,000 km (6,000 miles) from its winter quarters in southern Africa. The journey takes around four weeks, with males usually arriving first. Migrating swallows cover 200 miles a day, mainly during daylight, at speeds of up to 35 mph. They return to their wintering grounds in September and October.

Swallows usually live between four to eight years and return to the same traditional nesting area each year, often refurbishing an existing nest. There are instances where nests have been reused for nearly 50 years by successive generations. Swallows usually nest close to man, constructing nests of locally collected mud lined with feathers. Nests are usually located on the beams, ledges or other flat surfaces within buildings such as

Swallow

barns, outbuildings, sheds or garages, where they are protected from the weather. Any suitable building that has flight access may be used. Swallows have been known to use the exterior of a building where the overhang is sufficient to supply protection from the elements, although this is uncommon. Swallows depend on nearby habitats for their insect food and, as a rule, do not nest in the centre of large towns or cities.

1.2.3 House martins

The house martin (*Delichon urbica*) also covers great distances to reach the shores of the UK, with their winter range being in tropical Africa. They are found across the UK, except in parts of Scotland, and are here, typically, from mid-April until October.

Before man provided shelter, martins were cliff and cave dwellers. Unlike swallows, house martins do not need to enter into buildings, but make their nests under the eaves. Over many years house martins have become reliant on this close association with people, which has allowed them to inhabit even urban areas.

They nest in colonies, with an average group size of four to five nests, and nests are frequently used for several years, often by the same birds. The nest is made of pellets of mud lined with feathers and vegetable fibre.

House martin

House martins are short-lived, and most birds only breed for one year, though a few can have five or six breeding seasons.

As with swifts and swallows, house martins feed on the wing, consuming insects, such as flies, beetles and aphids. They can often be seen feeding at great heights in association with swifts.

Although declining in many localities, the house martin remains a familiar bird. There is evidence to suggest that the population has declined by 25–50%, but it is a difficult species to monitor and so the true picture remains unclear. House martins used to thrive in towns and cities, but are vanishing from them.

Indeed, all three of these insect-eating summer migrants have suffered declines and are of conservation concern. The causes are factors that affect them all to a greater or lesser degree: localised weather patterns and wider climate change; a reduction in the number of insects due to changes in land use; and losses of nest sites. The latter is something that is easy to remedy and will be an important aspect of the campaign to reverse their declining numbers.

1.2.4 House sparrows

House sparrow

House sparrows (*Passer domesticus*) are familiar resident birds throughout much of the UK and were once so common that it was easy to take them for granted. However, in recent years they have undergone a fast rate of decline, in the order of 62%, and they are now struggling to maintain their population in the UK. These declines have led to them being placed in the category of highest conservation concern. In built-up areas, the lack of suitable insect food for nestlings and a shortage of nest sites are thought to be contributing to the decline, although the reasons are not yet fully understood.

The house sparrow has a varied diet that includes seeds, nuts, berries, buds and bird-table food, but insects are important during spring and summer if populations are to be maintained.

Sparrows are colonial nesters and show a preference for nesting in holes or crevices in buildings, but they also use other opportunities. If there is a shortage of holes, they can build a free-standing nest in a thick hedge or conifer, although this rarely happens in the UK. The nest is an untidy structure, often comprising dry grass or straw lined with paper, feathers, string and similar miscellaneous items. They will readily use nest boxes and designs are available for incorporation into built structures. Pairs are faithful to their nest site and to each other for life.

1.2.5 Starlings

Starlings (*Sturnus vulgaris*) are also resident birds that, while still widespread in the UK (absent only from the Scottish highlands), have suffered a serious decline.

Adult starlings are adaptable when feeding and their diet can include a wide range of food, from naturally found items, such as insects, worms, snails, berries and fruit, to food offered on a garden bird table, especially those containing fat. Importantly for their young, there is no substitute in their diet for invertebrates, which is their sole food source.

Long-term monitoring by the British Trust for Ornithology (BTO) reveals a reduction in starling numbers in Britain by 66% since the mid-1970s. As a result of this decline in numbers, the starling is listed in the highest category of conservation concern. The reasons for this decline are thought to be the loss of permanent pasture and mixed farming, and the increased use of farm chemicals and an associated reduction in their staple food of earthworms and leather jackets, particularly on arable land. Another important factor is a shortage of nesting sites in many parts of the UK.

Starling

1.2.6 Barn owls

From the middle of the nineteenth century, the barn owl (*Tyto alba*) began to decline in Britain as a result of persecution. Unfortunately, the decline continued due to a number of factors, including changing farming practices, harsh winter weather, road casualties, the use of pesticides, and a reduction in hunting and nesting sites. The first reliable survey of barn owls in Britain was carried out during the 1990s as a collaboration between the British Trust for Ornithology and the Hawk and Owl Trust, and estimated the population at only 3,500 to 4,000 pairs, although there is some hope that the population has not declined further since then.

Barn owls hunt mainly from the air, rather than from a perch. The proximity of a good foraging area is important and barn owls can utilise any area of open habitat (not woodland) that supports small mammal populations. Permanent, rough, tussocky grassland is their optimum foraging habitat. Landscape suitability maps that cover all of England, Scotland and Wales may be found at the Barn Owl Trust website (www.barnowltrust.org.uk).

Given its name, it is no surprise to learn that the barn owl is a species for which buildings are important. It is thought that before this close association with man-made features formed, they used hollow trees or crevices in rocks. The species' association with human settlements is not recent, and evidence of this relationship has been found at iron-age and roman sites. In Britain the vast majority of occupied sites are agricultural buildings, particularly old stone, cob or brick-built barns and stock sheds. However, with many of these falling into decay or being converted, barn owls will make use of any building that meets their main requirements, including new build.

Barn owls generally use tall buildings, and entrance holes, roost perches and nests are usually over 3 m above ground level. Barn owls do not build a nest as such, but usually lay their eggs on a layer of owl pellets. Provided that they can remain out of sight within a building, they are not likely to be flushed out and will readily become accustomed to sounds associated with human, industrial or agricultural activity.

Unlike barn owls in mainland Europe, British barn owls do not live in urban areas. However, they are found in rural villages and on the urban fringe.

Barn owl

1.2.7 Peregrine falcons

The peregrine falcon (*Falco peregrinus*) is an amazing aerial predator, holding the record of being the fastest animal in the world, reaching speeds over 320 km per hour (200 mph) during its hunting dive. As a predator, peregrines are found at low densities, although they are widespread in the UK.

Peregrines have a generalist diet, but wherever there are feral pigeons these are their favoured prey. A wide range of birds are taken as prey, ranging in size from the goldcrest to the grey heron, and can, infrequently, also include mammals such as bats, as well as amphibians, lizards and large insects.

The nest site, known as an eyrie, is most often on a cliff ledge, quarry or other inaccessible and undisturbed location, but buildings and other constructions are increasingly being used for nesting. The nest itself is a slight scrape in any earth or old debris on the nest ledge, with no material brought in to build a nest.

Peregrine numbers suffered a sharp decline during the nineteenth and twentieth centuries due to illegal killing by humans. In addition, toxic agricultural chemicals, such as DDT, led to the collapse of the peregrine population in the UK in the late 1950s. The ban on the use of these toxic chemicals allowed the peregrine population to start a slow recovery. Currently this recovery is at a point where pre-decline levels have been reached over parts of their range (distribution) in the UK. However, recovery has been slow in other parts of the range and is now contracting again in northern Scotland.

Peregrine falcon

1.3 Living roofs and walls

Living roofs and walls have been more widely adopted in America and other European countries, although major cities in the UK are now starting to follow suit. Living roofs and walls can form an important element of sustainable building by reducing the risk of flooding, reducing the extremes of temperature fluctuation in a building and by providing enhancement for biodiversity. Much has already been written about the benefits and pitfalls of these features, and so Chapter 3, on designing for biodiversity, will only provide an overview, while directing the reader to much more extensive publications on the subject.

chapter two

Legislation, policy and regulations

This chapter provides an overview of wildlife and planning legislation, the Biodiversity Action Planning Process and the Building Regulations. The intention is to illustrate the processes and common areas that link legislation, policy and regulations together, and then view the whole picture in the context of the theme of this book. It is, however, natural that some readers may wish to explore certain aspects in more depth and so alongside the key facts there are links to further sources of information.

2.1 Wildlife legislation and what it means

There is a range of wildlife legislation that applies to species that use buildings. This legislation falls into two types:

1. To protect those species that have been deemed sufficiently vulnerable to require either protection under national legislation or from European Directives which have subsequently been implemented into UK law. Some species, such as all bat species, are protected by both and are commonly referred to as European Protected Species (EPS).
2. There is also legislation that emphasises the need to maintain and enhance biodiversity.

Importantly, this book deals with enhancing biodiversity by providing potential roosting and nesting sites that low or zero carbon buildings are otherwise unlikely to support. Before we concentrate on enhancement for biodiversity, it is important that we outline the role of the legislation that protects the species in question when they are already present and likely to be adversely affected by development proposals. Table 2.1 provides a list of the legislation most likely to apply to species associated with buildings. Table 2.2 explores, in uncomplicated terms, the most common application of this key legislation as it relates to wildlife and buildings.

Table 2.1: UK wildlife legislation relevant to biodiversity in buildings

England	Wales	Scotland	Northern Ireland
Wildlife and Countryside Act 1981 (as amended)			Wildlife NI Order 1985 (as amended)
Conservation (Natural Habitats & c) Regulations 1994 (as amended)			Nature Conservation and Amenity Lands (NI) Order 1985 (as amended)
Countryside and Rights of Way Act 2000		The Nature Conservation (Scotland) Act 2004	
Natural Environment and Rural Communities Act 2006			The Conservation (Natural Habitats etc.) Regulations (NI) 1995 (as amended)
			Environment (Northern Ireland) Order 2002

Table 2.2: The UK's main wildlife legislation in practical terms

Legislation	Application
Wildlife and Countryside Act 1981 (as amended)	This is the principal wildlife legislation in Great Britain for birds and includes the protection of certain species and the places they use for shelter and protection. All wild birds, their nests and eggs are, with few exceptions, fully protected by law. In addition, over 80 species or groups of species are given special protection under Schedule 1 of the Wildlife and Countryside Act 1981 (as amended).
	The Act makes it an offence to intentionally kill, injure or take any wild bird or their eggs or to take damage or destroy the nest while that nest is in use or being built (with the exception of a small number of birds listed under Schedule 2).
	Special penalties may be awarded for any offences related to birds listed on Schedule 1 of the Act (which include the peregrine falcon and barn owl) for which there are additional offences of disturbing these birds at their nests, or their dependent young.
	The maximum penalty that can be imposed for an offence in respect of a single bird, nest or egg is a fine of up to £5,000 and/or six months' imprisonment.
	The Act also gives some protection for bats and roosts in England and Wales, such as for intentional or reckless obstruction of access to a roost, but for practical purposes the protection of bats and their roosts now falls mostly under the Habitats Regulations.
Conservation (Natural Habitat & c) Regulations 1994 (as amended)	The Habitats Regulations derive from the EU Directive 92/43/EEC on the Conservation of Natural Habitats and of Wild Fauna and Flora 1992 and Council Directive 79/409/EEC on the conservation of wild birds. The Habitats Regulations implement these Directives into British law. This legislation affords protection to a range of species termed 'European Protected Species' (EPS). EPS include all species of bats.
	Under Regulation 39 it is an offence for anyone to intentionally kill, injure or take any wild bat, or sell, offer or expose for sale any live or dead bat. It is also an offence to damage or destroy any place used by bats for shelter or as a breeding site. A further offence is to deliberately or recklessly disturb a bat in a way that would affect its ability to survive, breed, rear young or affect the local distribution or abundance of the species.
	The potential fine for each offence is £5,000 and, if more than one bat is involved, £5,000 per bat. An offender can also be imprisoned for six months. The forfeiture of any bat by the court is mandatory on conviction, and items used to commit the offence – vehicles, for example – may be forfeited.
Countryside and Rights of Way Act 2000	For protected species, this Act strengthens the existing wildlife legislation by clarifying the wording of what constitutes an offence and the severity of penalties.
Natural Environment and Rural Communities Act 2006	This legislation places a statutory duty on all public bodies in England and Wales that each must, in exercising their functions, have regard, so far as is consistent with the proper exercise of those functions, to the purpose of conserving biodiversity (Section 40).
	Section 41 of the Act requires the Secretary of State to publish a list of habitats and species which are of principal importance for the conservation of biodiversity. The list has been drawn up in consultation with Natural England, as required by the Act.
	The Section 41 list (UK List of Priority Species and Habitats) is used to guide decision makers such as public bodies, including local and regional authorities, in implementing their duty under Section 40 of the Act, to have regard to the conservation of biodiversity in England, when carrying out their normal functions.
	There are 943 species of principal importance included on the Section 41 list. These are the species which have been identified as requiring action under the UK Biodiversity Action Plan and include the house sparrow, starling and seven species of bat – of which four are particularly reliant on buildings for roosts (greater and lesser horseshoe, soprano pipistrelle and brown long-eared bats).
The Nature Conservation (Scotland) Act 2004	In Scotland, it is the duty of every public body and office holder, in exercising any functions, to further the conservation of biodiversity so far as is consistent with the proper exercise of those functions.

For activities that would otherwise be illegal, but where a valid justification exists, European Protected Species licences can be issued. However, these can only be granted if the licensing authority is satisfied that the activity is preserving public health or public safety, or if there are other imperative reasons of overriding public interest. It must also be satisfied that there is no satisfactory alternative, and that the action authorised will not be detrimental to the maintenance of the population of the species concerned at a favourable conservation status in their natural range (i.e. affect the long-term distribution and abundance of its populations within the area). These licences are issued by Natural England in England, the Welsh Assembly Government for Wales, the Scottish Government Rural Directorate in Scotland, and the Environment and Heritage Service Northern Ireland.

For further details on species legislation, please refer to the following websites:

- Joint Nature Conservation Committee – www.jncc.gov.uk
- Department for Environment, Food and Rural Affairs – www.defra.gov.uk
- Natural England – www.naturalengland.org.uk
- The Welsh Assembly Government – http://new.wales.gov.uk
- The Scottish Government – www.scotland.gov.uk
- Northern Ireland Environment Agency – www.ehsni.gov.uk
- Bat Conservation Trust – www.bats.org.uk
- Royal Society for the Protection of Birds – www.rspb.org.uk

2.2 The planning process and biodiversity

The planning process is guided by its own set of legislation and regulations, and the most prominent of these are shown in Table 2.3.

Table 2.3: Planning legislation and policy in the UK

	England	Wales	Scotland	Northern Ireland
Planning legislation	Town and Country Planning Act 1990		Town and Country Planning (Scotland) Act 1997	The Planning (Northern Ireland) Order 1991 (as amended)
Planning regulations	The Town and Country Planning (Environmental Impact Assessment) (England and Wales) Regulations 1999 (SI 1999 No. 293)		The Environmental Impact Assessment (Scotland) Regulations 1999 (Scottish SI 1999 No. 1)	Planning (Environmental Impact Assessment) Regulations (Northern Ireland) 1999 (SR 1999 No. 73)
	The Environmental Assessment of Plans and Programmes Regulations 2004 (SI 2004 No. 1633)	The Environmental Assessment of Plans and Programmes (Wales) Regulations 2004 Welsh Statutory Instrument No.1656 (W.170)	The Environmental Assessment of Plans and Programmes (Scotland) Regulations 2004 (Scottish Statutory Instrument No. 258) Circular 2/2004: Strategic Environmental Assessment for Development Planning; The Environmental Assessment of Plans and Programmes (Scotland) Regulations 2004	The Environmental Assessment of Plans and Programmes Regulations (Northern Ireland) 2004 (Statutory Rule 2004 No. 280)

Requirements from the Government on the implementation of this legislation is given in a series of planning policy statements. In the UK we have the following documents advising planning officers how they should take nature conservation matters into account:

- In England, PPS 9 Biodiversity and Geological Conservation (ODPM, 2005b); Circular 06/2005 Biodiversity and Geological Conservation – Statutory Obligations and their Impact within the Planning System (ODPM, 2005a); Planning for Biodiversity and Geological Conservation: A Guide to Good Practice (ODPM, 2006) (see www.communities.gov.uk).
- In Wales, TAN5 Nature Conservation and Planning (http://new.wales.gov.uk).
- In Scotland, NPPG14 Natural Heritage and PAN60 Planning for Natural Heritage (www.scotland.gov.uk).
- In Northern Ireland, PPS2 Planning and Nature Conservation (www.ni-environment.gov.uk).

The planning legislation and terminology differ slightly in each country, but the principles are similar.

The important link between wildlife legislation and planning policy from the point of view of the biodiversity enhancements detailed in this book are those legislative requirements for the conservation and enhancement of biodiversity by local authorities.

Guidance exists for local authorities on carrying out this function in the form of the publication *Guidance for Local Authorities on implementing the Biodiversity Duty* (Defra, 2007; www.defra.gov.uk), although the most specific guidance is given in the legislation and regulations documents detailed above for each of the UK countries.

The biodiversity planning toolkit provides a one-stop service for all matters related to biodiversity in the planning process (www.biodiversityplanningtoolkit.com – planned launch spring 2010).

In order to give a picture of how the planning application process works with regard to the consideration of biodiversity, Table 2.4 maps the development process, biodiversity consideration and the planning process onto the stages of the Royal Institute of British Architects (RIBA) Outline Plan of Work.

As Table 2.4 illustrates, information showing how well or how adversely a development has impacted on priority species and habitats is reported by the local authority in their Annual Monitoring Report. A brief explanation of priority habitats and species, and the Biodiversity Action Plan reporting of which they form a part, now follows.

Table 2.4: RIBA Outline Plan of Work, showing at which stages biodiversity must be considered during a traditional procurement process

RIBA Work Stages

Stage A	Stage B	Stage C
Appraisal	Design brief	Concept

Development Process

Appraisal	Design
• Establish objectives	• Identify opportunities and constraints
• Design team selection	• Produce Masterplan
• Initial feasibility studies	• Prepare Section 106 agreement
• Land identification	• Detailed planning application
• Secure land purchase option	• Complete land purchase

Biodiversity consideration

Consultation and/or scoping study	
	Detailed survey and impact assessment
	Design of development to incorporate biodiversity objectives

Planning Process

	Pre-application guidance and advice on application type	Guidance and advice on application type

→ Process

Stage D	Stage E	Stage F	Stage G	Stage H	Stage J	Stage K	Stage L
Design development	Technical design	Production information	Tender documentation	Tender action	Mobilisation	Construction to practical completion	Post practical completion

Pre-construction
- Preparation of detailed production information (drawings, specifications etc.) to allow tenders to be sought
- Application for statutory approvals
- Tender returns and appraisal

Construction
- Award contract
- Construction works
- Divestiture of development

Use
- Ongoing monitoring and maintenance by management company
- Review of project performance in use

Prepare and agree enhancement, mitigation and compensation*

Implement agreed enhancement mitigation and compensation

Management, monitoring and aftercare

Validation and registration	Pre-decision assessment	Formal determination of planning application			Local Planning Authority issues planning consent	Compliance monitoring	Annual monitoring report, which includes reporting the effects of development consents on priority habitats and species

* If protected species are affected, then a licence to make the activities legal is required.

2.3 Biodiversity Action Plan reporting

In 1992, 153 nations signed the Convention on Biological Diversity at the Rio Earth Summit. As a result, a detailed plan for the protection of the UK's priority habitats and species was formed and Biodiversity Action Plans (BAPs) written for each. The BAPs set the targets and actions required. They also identified the partners who were needed to make it happen. These BAPs for priority species and habitats are produced at the national, regional and local level. The local level plans translate the national targets into local actions. Additional local plans are also produced for any species or habitats that are important at a local level.

It is biodiversity at the local level that local authorities have a duty to conserve and enhance. Within the Local Development Framework (LDF) guidance there is a requirement for local authorities to report annually against a series of Core Output Indicators. One such indicator is entitled 'Ways of assessing biodiversity change'. So losses and gains to biodiversity that are anticipated as a result of a proposed development must be reported on in detail as part of a planning application which the Local Planning Authority will consider when reaching its decision. If consented, the information on losses or gains to biodiversity is fed through the reporting system and will inform a feedback mechanism (see Figure 2.1) on the impact of the construction industry on biodiversity.

Figure 2.1 illustrates the feedback loop. A project working group, hosted by the Royal Town Planning Institute (RTPI) and involving representatives from industry, government advisory bodies and non-government wildlife organisations, is currently (2009) underway to make this complex reporting system easier to use, more effective and, as a result, more widely used than it is currently.

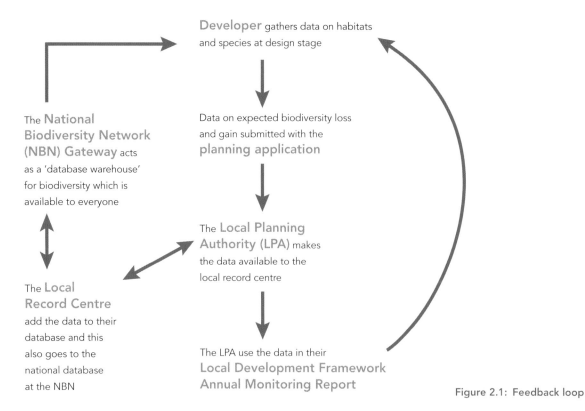

Figure 2.1: Feedback loop

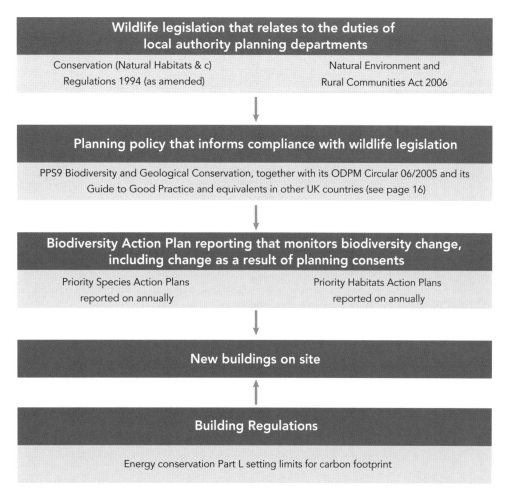

Wildlife legislation that relates to the duties of local authority planning departments

| Conservation (Natural Habitats & c) Regulations 1994 (as amended) | Natural Environment and Rural Communities Act 2006 |

Planning policy that informs compliance with wildlife legislation

PPS9 Biodiversity and Geological Conservation, together with its ODPM Circular 06/2005 and its Guide to Good Practice and equivalents in other UK countries (see page 16)

Biodiversity Action Plan reporting that monitors biodiversity change, including change as a result of planning consents

| Priority Species Action Plans reported on annually | Priority Habitats Action Plans reported on annually |

New buildings on site

Building Regulations

Energy conservation Part L setting limits for carbon footprint

Figure 2.2: Connection between wildlife legislation, planning policy and process and biodiversity in England

This section has illustrated the connection between wildlife legislation, planning policy and process and biodiversity reporting that are relevant to the enhancement measures made to buildings. This is shown diagrammatically in Figure 2.2.

The part of the diagram in Figure 2.2 yet to be covered, but of great importance, concerns the Building Regulations.

2.4 Building Regulations

The Building Regulations set standards for the design and construction of buildings in order to ensure the safety and health of people in or about those buildings. They also include requirements to ensure that fuel and power are conserved and that facilities are provided for people, including those with disabilities, to access and move around inside buildings. The relevant acts and regulations for the UK are shown in Table 2.5.

The Building Regulations for England and Wales are made under powers provided in the Building Act 1984. The current (2009) editions of the

Table 2.5: Acts and regulations for the UK

	Act	Regulations	Part relating to energy	Date last updated
England and Wales	Building Act 1984	Building Regulations 2000	Part L	2006
Scotland	Building (Scotland) Act 2003	Building (Scotland) Regulations 2004	Section 6	2007
Northern Ireland	Building Regulations (Northern Ireland) Order 1979	Building Regulations (Northern Ireland) 2000	Sections F1 and F2	2006

regulations are The Building Regulations 2000 (as amended) and The Building (Approved Inspectors etc.) Regulations 2000 (as amended), and the majority of building projects are required to comply with them.

The requirements with which building work should comply are contained in Schedule 1 to the Building Regulations and are grouped under 14 'parts', which include subjects such as fire safety, access, toxic substances, ventilation and, most importantly for this book, the conservation of fuel and power.

Approved Documents (ADs) are produced by the Government and give guidance on how the requirements of the Building Regulations can be satisfied. The guidance given in these ADs does not have to be followed, but if it is not, then it has to be demonstrated that the requirements have been satisfied by other means. The ADs are updated more often than the regulations themselves.

The ADs are published by National Building Specification (NBS) and paper versions can be purchased from the RIBA (www.ribabookshops.com) or they can be downloaded free from the Planning Portal website (www.planningportal.gov.uk).

There are four Approved Documents to Part L on the conservation of fuel and power, as follows.

Dwellings:
- Approved Document L1A: Conservation of fuel and power (New dwellings) (2006 edition).
- Approved Document L1B: Conservation of fuel and power (Existing dwellings) (2006 edition).

Buildings other than dwellings:
- Approved Document L2A: Conservation of fuel and power (New buildings other than dwellings) (2006 edition).
- Approved Document L2B: Conservation of fuel and power (Existing buildings other than dwellings) (2006 edition).

Part L underwent a major revision in 2006, and the drivers for the change included the Government's Energy White Paper commitment to raise the energy performance of buildings and the introduction of European legislation – the Energy Performance of Buildings Directive. Further revisions to Part L demanding increased energy efficiency are expected in 2010, 2013 and 2016. By 2016, all new homes must be zero carbon and there is an ambition for all new non-domestic buildings to be zero carbon by 2019.

In order to reach these targets, buildings must have sufficient thermal insulation to slow down the flow of heat from inside to outside. Ideally this insulation is continuous, with no gaps or thermal bridges for heat loss. U values give a measure of heat loss; the lower the U value, the smaller the loss of heat – so a low U value is a good U value. In short, there is a need for an 'air-tightness layer' to stop heat loss through leakage from occurring. This can be achieved in a number of ways depending on the design of the building and the materials used. So the difference between a low or zero carbon building and a conventional building will be the achievement of a very good U value and air-tightness.

In July 2009 the UK Government published *The UK Low Carbon Transition Plan: National Strategy for Climate and Energy.* This reconfirmed the Government's policy that all new homes will be zero carbon from 2016.

Unless biodiversity is considered early on in the design process, these ever more stringent demands for increased energy efficiency of buildings will lead to losses in the biodiversity that have shared our built environment for centuries. This book addresses this issue because if we do not, there will be very few, if any, future roosting opportunities for bats or nesting opportunities for birds in our buildings. Without these measures, key species will be adversely affected by new developments; not only meaning a failure to achieve truly sustainable building, but also an erosion of the quality of life we all hope to experience in our working and home environments.

chapter three

Designing for biodiversity in low and zero carbon buildings

This chapter highlights some general principles about nesting and roosting that should be considered when designing for biodiversity enhancement. It then considers some of the ready-made products for roosting and nesting that are on the market, before going on to explain how these, and bespoke roosting and nesting spaces, can be incorporated into low and zero carbon building design.

As this book is about biodiversity enhancement, specifically in low and zero carbon buildings, the importance of other environmental sustainability issues is recognised and this is reflected in the comments on a range of other associated topics that will be referred to in this chapter.

3.1 General principles

There are certain details about nesting and roosting that need to be considered. These will be related to the size of the provision, the size and location of the access to it, the aspect and height at which it is placed, the spacing between each, the materials it is made of, and its location in the context of features of the surrounding environment.

Looking at the needs of building-reliant species in a slightly wider context, it will always be important that they are able to find sufficient food within the range they can travel from the building in which they have their nesting/roosting provision. The range will vary between species, but it is worth noting that many of the species in question are insectivorous and so any habitat features nearby that host insects, such as rivers, ponds, unimproved grasslands, ancient semi-natural woodland and hedgerows planted with native vegetation, will all prove valuable if close at hand. Even species that can travel many kilometres will benefit from saving their energy and being able to feed closer to home.

Connectivity of the landscape is also important for a number of species, in particular slow-flying bat species. This refers to the natural (or man-made) features that offer cover and linkage around the built environment and throughout the surrounding habitats. This might be by moving from garden to garden via mature vegetation or hedges, or using these and other features, such as tree lines and river banks, to navigate. This is often referred to as 'green infrastructure' and is useful not only for the species covered by this book, but also by a whole host of other wildlife. It is often possible that these commuting routes for wildlife are shared by the human inhabitants in the form of footpaths, cycle ways, bridle paths, etc. Where this is the case, it is important to remember that for nocturnal wildlife, even the most suitable habitat as seen in the day can be made unavailable for nocturnal wildlife by artificial lighting. Chapter 4 deals with lighting and wildlife.

Table 3.1: General outline of roosting and nesting requirements

Bat/bird species	Access dimensions	Roost/nesting dimensions	Height of entry
Crevice-dwelling bats	15–20 mm (h) x 20–50 mm (w)	Any size as long as some components of the area are crevices about 20–30 mm as the width of the gap Greater total areas of about 1 sq m would be useful for nursery (summer) roosts Male roosts contain smaller numbers of bats or even individual bats Roof void dwelling bats need timber joists or beams on which to roost	2–7 m
Bats needing a flying area	15–20 mm (h) x 20–50 mm (w)	2–2.8 m (h) x 5 m (w) x 5 m (l) not trussed to allow flight. Ideally 2.8 m height, but a height of 2 m may be acceptable in some circumstances. To incorporate roost crevices dimensions as above with crevice-dwelling bats	Over 2 m
Horseshoe bats	Lesser horseshoes 300 mm (w) x 200 mm (h) Greater horseshoes 400 mm (w) x 300 mm (h)	2–2.8 m (h) x 5 m (w) x 5 m (l) not trussed to allow flight. Ideally 2.8 m height, but a height of 2 m may be acceptable in some circumstances	Over 2 m
Swifts	65 mm (w) x 30 mm (h)	400 mm (w) x 200 mm (d) x 150 mm (h). Can be slightly smaller	Over 5 m above ground and away from obstructions and creepers. Preferably integral to the building, but where this is not possible external, e.g. under the eaves. It is important to have several potential nest sites for swifts in one area
House sparrow	32 mm diameter round hole	350 mm (h) x 150 mm (w) x 150 mm (d)	Ideally within the structure at soffit/eaves level, but otherwise as an external box at this same location. At least 3 m high for starlings and 2 m for sparrows
Starling	45 mm round hole	400 mm (h) x 180 mm (w) x 180 mm (d)	
House martin	25 mm (h) x 60–65 mm (w)	180 mm diameter	Precast nests are available and should be placed underneath the eaves, but not directly above windows or doors at a height of at least 5 m
Swallow	To access the interior of a building, swallows require a gap of 50 mm (h) x 70 mm (w)	Nesting platform 100 mm (d) x 260 mm (w)	Precast nests are available or nesting platforms can be made. These should be placed on a ledge inside a building at 1.5 m or more where droppings will not be a nuisance
Barn owls	130 mm (w) x 250 mm (h) into building 130 mm (w) x 130 mm (h) into internal box where these are provided	600 mm (h) x 400 mm (w) x 400 mm (d)	Over 3 m
Peregrine falcons	Open air	A shallow tray with raised edges, optionally containing substrate such as gravel or pea shingle and compost or woodchips, secured to a sheltered ledge on the structure: 450 mm (l) x 600 mm (w) x 40 mm (h). Or a box 450 mm (l) x 600 mm (w) x 900 mm (h) can be provided	Over 20 m

Aspect of roost	Temperature °C		Materials and other comments
	Summer	Winter	
Summer nursery roosts on most southerly or westerly aspect for solar heating	30–40 (daytime)	0–6	Rough (for grip)
			Non-toxic or corrosive
Male roosts and winter hibernation roosts on northerly aspect			No risk of entanglement
			Suitable thermal properties (reducing 24-hour fluctuations), but allowing maximum thermal gain for summer roosts
			Access not lit by artificial lighting
The crevice-roosting provision within the roost to be located on the south or west side for solar heating. The flight area not as important	30–40	0–6	
The roost is most likely to be in a roof space and this should have an orientation that allows a south-facing solar gain or, better still, an L-shape to allow temperature-range choice	30–40	6–10	
In shade, out of direct sunlight and away from windows	Avoid direct sun that would lead to over-heating		Boxes made from concrete, masonry or marine ply or else compartments created within a suitable part of the building
			In establishing a new colony, playing recorded swift calls is extremely useful to aid their finding the site
Out of direct sun. Easterly is best			
Out of direct sunlight. Preferably east facing. Not over the main living area as the birds can be noisy			Several nest provisions 1.5 m apart
North or east facing. Avoid positioning where droppings will be an issue			Swallows and house martins require a source of damp mud in order to construct their nests
			Swallow nests should not be placed close together. House martins are colonial in their nesting, so several nests together will prove attractive to them
No requirement			
Facing away from prevailing winds and towards open countryside	No requirement		Internal boxes softwood shuttering ply or similar
			No sharp edges
			Where access is through a vertical structure, a ledge on which to land to gain access to the roofspace and/or roost is important unless the gap is large enough for flight
Not located on a part of the building that would face full sun to prevent over-heating of eggs and young. North or north-east is best. Away from human disturbance and prevailing winds	No requirement, except avoiding full sun		Solid surface

This book is not intended to take the place of an ecologist and it is expected that the choice of provision for enhancing the biodiversity of built structures, and how that is accommodated within any development, will be guided by an experienced ecologist (website details for ecologist organisations are given at the end of this book). It is always preferable to get a recommendation for similar work undertaken.

Table 3.1 takes principles about the dimensions, internal conditions and location of roost and nest provision, and gives some general indications of requirements.

3.1.1 Ready-made products – general principles

There are a number of products available that provide roosting or nesting potential either as a feature to be incorporated into the building or as attachments to it. This book concentrates on those that are designed to be an integral part of the building. These range in price from under £15 to over £80 each, with most in the region of £30 to £40. It is recognised that the author may be unaware of some available ready-made products and therefore it cannot be claimed that the products reviewed are an exhaustive list.

Ready-made products are available for some, but not all, of the species discussed in this chapter of the book. Where relevant, a critique of these products is supplied from a construction point of view. Unfortunately, it is not yet possible to make an evaluation based on the extent of use of these products by the wildlife for which they were intended, as often the data on the degree of uptake have not been collected or not enough time has elapsed to give a verdict. The importance of monitoring uptake cannot be overstated. It is only by feedback on success, or otherwise, that future designs and recommendations can be effective.

There are some general points that relate to the size of the product and the ease with which it can be incorporated within any construction. For example, if made in the UK by a brick or stone manufacturer, then it is likely to fit either UK brick or stone measures. Products from outside the UK will fit the standard construction sizes for the country in question, which differ from those in the UK and so work is required to accommodate them. If designed by species specialists, these may not be to a standard size.

Solutions to some common problems regarding dimensions and ready-made products are given in Table 3.2. Table 3.3 outlines the advantages of and considerations for materials used in ready-made products.

Table 3.2: Solutions to common problems regarding dimensions and ready-made products

Problem	Solution
Width out of coordination	Increase widths of perpend joint in brickwork either side and/or above and below to fit, or add fired clay tiles to maintain 10 mm joints
Height out of coordination	Turn bricks on edge underneath or on end and cut soldier course to length
Depth out of coordination	No easy solution – likely to cause thermal bridge through the U value envelope and bridge cavities in cavity wall requiring cavity tray
Width and height out of coordination	Do not use brickwork, but instead use blockwork and render or insulated render so it is possible to conceal the necessary correction measures under render
Width, height and depth out of coordination	No easy solution – consider a different product or method of construction

Table 3.3: Advantages of and considerations for materials used in ready-made products

Material		Advantages	Considerations
Clay facing brick		Frost resistant Strong Thermal mass Durable	Absorbent of moisture including urine High embodied energy
Cement-based concrete		Cement is impervious to moisture Strong Durable Thermal mass	High embodied energy High embodied carbon Alkali – do not use aluminium fasteners
Cement and wood chip fibre concrete		Thermal mass Added moisture mass Medium carbon sequestration Vapour permeable Easy to mould to any shape 50-year track record	Wood will absorb moisture and urine Medium embodied energy Medium embodied carbon Alkali – do not use aluminium fasteners
Plywood	INT – internal plywood	Carbon sequestration during growth INT suitable for internal construction	INT not suitable for damp, humid conditions Unsuitable in the presence of urine
	WBP – weather and boil proof (exterior)	Carbon sequestration during growth External – suitable for external construction WBP suitable for damp, humid conditions Likely to be suitable in the presence of urine	
	Marine grade ply	Carbon sequestration during growth Made for yacht making Much more than required for building applications Check for the BSI Kitemark to ensure product is as specified	
Cement and wood particle board		Standard building product Fire protection High thermal mass Medium carbon sequestration (wood particles) Tough Durable Low moisture permeability (cement) Uncut cement surfaces will resist water absorption	Wood particles will absorb moisture on cut edges Tough on carpentry tools Alkali – do not use aluminium fasteners Surface hard and smooth – needs roughening for climbing and hanging
Softwood		Carbon sequestration during growth Readily available locally Reclaimed and reused scraps can be used Easy to work Easy on tools Douglas Fir is naturally durable	Most not durable and wood preservatives cannot be used Choose reclaimed, locally grown or FSC temperate species
Hard wood		Carbon sequestration during growth Readily available locally Reclaimed and reused scraps can be used Easy to work (old oak is hard work) Easy on tools (old oak is hard on tools) Most UK hardwoods are naturally durable Most UK hardwoods do not require preservatives	New acidic timber will stain a building with tannin New acidic timber will stain steel fasteners and vice versa Ideally need stainless steel fasteners (not as cheap as steel) Details of box need to be self-draining (roof and floor) away from a building Choose reclaimed, locally grown or FSC temperate species

Table 3.4: Thermal insulation of ready-made products

	Advantages	Considerations
None of the pre-made boxes considered are insulated, so if they breach the U value envelope of low or zero carbon buildings they need to be wrapped in thermal insulation* and linked to the U value envelope to maintain its integrity	This can be allowed for during the design process	This has to be done in such a way as to preserve the integrity of the U value envelope

* Features of thermal insulation materials:
  Foamed glass has high thermal mass and moisture/vapour resistance
  Rock mineral fibre has low thermal/acoustic mass and is air/vapour permeable – performance is diminished if moist, hydrophobic (rejects water)
  Slag mineral fibre has low thermal/acoustic mass and is air/vapour permeable – performance is diminished if moist, hydrophobic (rejects water)
  Glasswool has low thermal/acoustic mass and is air/vapour permeable – performance is diminished if moist hydrophobic (rejects water)
  Expanded polystyrene has low thermal/acoustic mass and can reject moisture
  Cellulose fibre is hygroscopic and will absorb moisture without loss of performance
  Dense wood fibre is hygroscopic and will absorb moisture without loss of performance, and the high thermal/acoustic mass will protect from solar radiation, but hold heat longer
  Plastics – avoid the risk of off-gassing, low thermal/acoustic mass, not hygroscopic, not normally breathing
  A more comprehensive comparison is available on the GreenSpec website (www.greenspec.co.uk)

Table 3.5: Air-tightness of ready-made products

	Advantages	Considerations
Air-tightness is unlikely to have been a high priority in the design and manufacture of these products, so if they breach the U value envelope of low to zero carbon buildings they need to be wrapped in an air-tightness layer (ATL) and linked to the U value envelope's ATL in order to maintain its integrity.	This can be allowed for during the design process. Bat box joints can be taped over. Natural paper-based ATLs are available. Natural adhesives are available.	This has to be done in such a way as to preserve the integrity of the U value envelope.

Tables 3.4 and 3.5 explain the advantages and considerations regarding thermal insulation and the air-tightness of ready-made products.

To support manufacturers, designers and DIY bat and bird box makers, GreenSpec has developed a spreadsheet to help determine the sizes of boxes to coordinate with masonry sizes. The aim is to try to work with masonry sizes to avoid disruptive working, to maintain the aesthetics of fairfaced masonry, and to avoid cutting and material waste. Numerous issues are addressed, such as:

- co-ordinating with brick, block and stone;
- accounting for the fact that UK and EU masonry block dimensions differ;
- the fact that UK was imperial, has been modular and now uses metric bricks;
- jointing may be imperial, 10 mm or thin joint;

- building in, or installing into, built openings requires different sizes; and
- insulation may need to be accommodated around the box.

The spreadsheet gives instant sizes and provides guidance on the space left inside for bat/bird accommodation. The spreadsheet is on the GreenSpec website (www.greenspec.co.uk).

Having looked at the general principles that apply to ready-made products, this book now examines the provision for each species or species group in turn. For each, any ready-made products (where these are available) will be reviewed. Section 3.12 then illustrates the integration of these products or bespoke spaces for roosting or nesting into a range of building types.

3.2 Crevice-dwelling bats

Crevice-dwelling bats is an arbitrary category that covers a wide range of species that tend to select roosts which could be described as a crevices or narrow gaps. This might be the area in traditional houses that is found between the roofing felt and tiles, or under hanging tiles or the weather boarding on the exterior of a building, or in gaps in the woodwork within a roof space, such as mortise joints. The expanse of the crevice might be small or cover a large area, but what these bats have in common is the preference to roost somewhere where they can retreat from open spaces. This category also includes bat species which may be visible when entering a roof space and require timber joists or beams on which to roost (roof-void dwelling bats). The species in question are: Common pipistrelle, soprano pipistrelle, Nathusius' pipistrelle (pipistrelle species most often hidden from view), Brandt's, whiskered, noctule, serotine, Leisler's, Daubenton's, barbastelle and Bechstein's. Table 3.6 lists some considerations for crevice-dwelling bats.

Table 3.6: Considerations and key requirements for crevice-dwelling bats

Consideration	Solution
Where in a development	Anywhere that the access is not illuminated by artificial lighting
Where in a building	Summer nursery roosts in most southerly or westerly aspect for solar heating
	Male roosts and winter hibernation roosts on northerly aspect
Height	Between 2–7 m
Dimensions	Any size as long as some components of the area are crevices in the region of 20–30 mm as the width of gap
	Greater total area of this crevice provision of about 1 sq m would be useful for nursery (summer) roosts
	Male roosts contain a smaller number of bats or even individual bats
Access dimensions	15–20 mm (h) x 20–50 mm (w)
Other considerations	Rough (for grip)
	Non-toxic and non-corrosive
	No risk of entanglement
	Suitable thermal properties (reducing 24-hour fluctuations), but allowing maximum thermal gain for summer roosts (thermal mass)
	Access not lit by artificial lighting

Bat Access Tile Set
Tudor Roof Tile Co. Limited

TYPE OF PRODUCT: Bat access tiles

WEBSITE: www.tudorrooftiles.co.uk

WHERE USED: On a roof slope in place of standard tiles

PRODUCT INFORMATION: Texture – Natural Clay (without sand face) or Sandface

5 Tudor colours and natural clay

PRODUCT USE: For use within the roof tiles – the top 'tunnel' tile offers the bat an 18 mm (h) x 165 mm (l) (approx.) tunnel to an entrance hole in the undertiles. This allows the bat to crawl into the roost area

(see Drawings Nos 1, 3, 5, 6, 9, 10 and 19, pp. 40, 55, 59, 61, 65, 67 and 83, respectively)

Advantages			Considerations			
Familiar material	✓		Unfamiliar material; unsure how to protect	N/A		
Easy to install	✓		Thermal bridges	N/A (but does create opening)		
Durable	✓		Exposed wood particles on cut or damaged edges may absorb moisture	N/A		
Low or no maintenance	✓		Must be maintained with 'special' unfamiliar paint	N/A		
Frost resistant	✓		Embodied energy	Medium		
Thermal mass	Medium or high		Embodied carbon	Depends on fuel used		
Fits UK construction sizes	✓		Degree of fit to UK construction sizes	✓ ✓ ✓ (fits all 3 dimensions)		
			Product uptake	Unknown		

Other
- Could be used scattered across a roof slope or on different roof slopes
- Ridge entry tile available – this may form a roost area too or provide access to one (see Drawing No. 5)
- Use in uninsulated sloping roofs will act as roof vents

Other
- Standard tile set is designed for roof slopes and can be placed above, at, or below eaves triangles, over the roof slope generally or at the ridge triangle
- Supported lapped underlay and aperture through underlay to give access to roof space

Ibstock Bat Roost Entrance Arch Brick
Ibstock

TYPE OF PRODUCT:	Bat roost entrance brick
WEBSITE:	www.ibstock.com
WHERE USED:	In place of a normal single brick – bed joint omitted for middle two-thirds of brick
PRODUCT INFORMATION:	Fired clay brick – size 65 mm (h) x 215 mm (w) x 102 mm (d)
PRODUCT USE:	Allows bats to pass through the outer leaf to the cavity of the wall or to spaces provided beyond

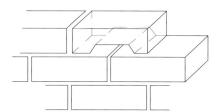 

Advantages		Considerations	
Familiar material	✓	Unfamiliar material; unsure how to protect	N/A
Easy to install	✓	Thermal bridges	N/A but does create opening
Durable	✓	Exposed wood particles on cut or damaged edges may absorb moisture	N/A
Low or no maintenance	N/A	Must be maintained with 'special' unfamiliar paint	N/A
Frost resistant	✓	Embodied energy	Medium
Thermal mass	Medium or high	Embodied carbon	Depends on fuel used
Fits UK construction sizes	✓	Degree of fit to UK construction sizes	✓ ✓ ✓ (fits all 3 dimensions)
		Product uptake	Unknown

Other
- Could be used as an access via eaves into the roof voids
- Fairfaced, no need for rendering over
- Versatile: can be used in pairs for bird root access or in multiples creating larger openings (see Barn Owl Drawing No. 2)

Other
- Only a passage, not a roost
- Only suitable for uninsulated cavity walls which should not feature in future low and zero carbon buildings except to unoccupied, uninsulated attic spaces or out-buildings

RoofBLOCK
RoofBLOCK

TYPE OF PRODUCT:	Bat roost – concrete eaves/verge system
WEBSITE:	www.roofblock.co.uk
WHERE USED:	Flat, hipped or any pitch roof – outer leaf of cavity wall or half brick extension of solid wall
PRODUCT INFORMATION:	Made from recycled aggregates and eco-cement
PRODUCT USE:	Block with bat slit to allow access to the hollow block section of
	(see Drawing Nos 2 and 6, pp. 54 and 61)

Advantages		Considerations	
Familiar material	✓	Unfamiliar material; unsure how to protect	N/A
Easy to install	Must be designed in	Thermal bridges	Risk of thermal bridge through thin cavity wall construction – can be improved with wider insulated cavity (see below)
Durable	✓	Exposed wood particles on cut or damaged edges may absorb moisture	N/A
Low or no maintenance	✓	Must be maintained with 'special' unfamiliar paint	N/A
Frost resistant	✓	Embodied energy	Medium
Thermal mass	High	Embodied carbon	Low (EcoCement)
Fits UK construction sizes	✓	Degree of fit to UK construction sizes	✓ ✓ (see Table 3.2)
		Product uptake	Unknown

Other
- Numerous endorsements and accolades
- Roosts can be positioned on any elevation unobtrusively
- Potentially large capacity roosts if adjacent blocks made available and linked
- Made for cavity walls, but will fit on half brick extension of 1B solid wall
- Fairfaced, no need for rendering over

Other
- Reduces U value locally, in wider cavity wall construction with full fill cavity insulation
- Profile may need to be modified with thicker walls and thicker insulation (see Drawing No. 6)
- Eco-cement should have less embodied carbon
- Recycled aggregates are likely to have less embodied energy and/or carbon

Ibstock Enclosed Bat Box
Ibstock

TYPE OF PRODUCT: Bat roost

WEBSITE: www.ibstock.com

WHERE USED: Replaces three or four bricks in stackbond in cavity wall construction

PRODUCT INFORMATION: Fired clay brick slip face – available for all brick types and with option of bat design. Bat motif: durable metallic, set in face of box

Sizes 215 mm (w) x 215 mm (h) x 102mm (d), or 215 mm (w) x 290 mm (h) x 102 mm (d)

PRODUCT USE: Creates several roosting zones inside the box – roost contained within product

(see Drawing Nos 7 and 8, pp. 62 and 63)

  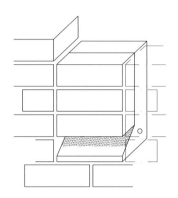

Enclosed Bat Box C

Advantages		Considerations	
Familiar material	✓	Unfamiliar material; unsure how to protect	N/A
Easy to install	✓	Thermal bridges	N/A
Durable	✓	Exposed wood particles on cut or damaged edges may absorb moisture	N/A
Low or no maintenance	✓	Must be maintained with 'special' unfamiliar paint	N/A
Frost resistant	✓	Embodied energy	High
Thermal mass	Medium or high	Embodied carbon	High
Fits UK construction sizes	✓	Degree of fit to UK construction sizes	✓ ✓ ✓ (fits all 3 dimensions)
		Product uptake	Unknown

Other
- Could be used in multiples (but lintel required if side by side)

Other
- May absorb urine, which in time may result in localised odour

Forticrete Bat Box
Forticrete

TYPE OF PRODUCT:	Bat roost
WEBSITE:	www.forticrete.co.uk
WHERE USED:	In outer-wall construction
PRODUCT INFORMATION:	Cast-stone front face
	Bat silhouette plaque cast into face
	Backing – high grade plywood that is sawn and roughened internally for bat use
	Maintenance free
	Sizes: 215 mm (h) x 440 mm (w) x 100 mm (d) overall (depth comprises 65 mm cast stone and 35 mm plywood)
	Bespoke sizes and designs available to special order
PRODUCT USE:	Roost contained within product

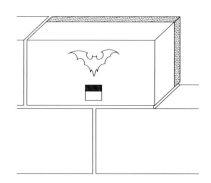

Advantages			Considerations			
Familiar material	✓		Unfamiliar material; unsure how to protect	N/A		
Easy to install	✓		Thermal bridges	N/A		
Durable	✓		Exposed wood particles on cut or damaged edges may absorb moisture	N/A		
Low or no maintenance	✓		Must be maintained with 'special' unfamiliar paint	N/A		
Frost resistant	✓		Embodied energy	High		
Thermal mass	Medium or high		Embodied carbon	High		
Fits UK construction sizes	✓		Degree of fit to UK construction sizes	✓ ✓ ✓ (fits all 3 dimensions)		
			Product uptake	Unknown		

Other
- Could be used in a multiple arrangement with mortared purpend between (but lintel required if side by side)
- Fairfaced, so no need for rendering over

Other

Norfolk Bat Brick
Norfolk Bat Group

TYPE OF PRODUCT: Bat roost

WEBSITE: www.norfolk-bat-group.org.uk

WHERE USED: In bridges, tunnels and similar structures

PRODUCT INFORMATION: Size – brick-sized, approximately
70 mm (h) x 200 mm (w) x 100 mm (d)

Hand-made of absorbent clay, roughened with sand and
fired to about 1,100°C to make them frost-proof. They have a
series of appropriate sized slits on the face

PRODUCT USE: Provides the right conditions for hibernating bats, such
as Daubenton's, Natterer's, Brown Long-eared, Brandts,
Whiskered and Barbastelle

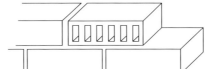

Advantages			Considerations			
Familiar material	✓		Unfamiliar material; unsure how to protect	N/A		
Easy to install	✓		Thermal bridges	N/A		
Durable	✓		Exposed wood particles on cut or damaged edges may absorb moisture	N/A		
Low or no maintenance	✓		Must be maintained with 'special' unfamiliar paint	N/A		
Frost resistant	✓		Embodied energy	High		
Thermal mass	Medium or high		Embodied carbon	Depends on fuel used		
Fits UK construction sizes	✓		Degree of fit to UK construction sizes	✓ ✓ ✓ (fits all 3 dimensions)		
Product uptake	Known to be well used by bats Recommended structures such as arches, tunnels, and bridges where crevices are in short supply		Unknown product uptake	N/A Not designed for, and generally not suitable for, low and zero carbon buildings		

Other
- Could be used in multiples (but lintel may be required)

Other
- These are not designed as access bricks

Schwegler Bat Roost Range
Schwegler GmbH

TYPE OF PRODUCT: Bat roost

WEBSITE: www.schwegler-nature.com

WHERE USED: In outer-wall construction

PRODUCT INFORMATION: Durable, weather-resistant and air-permeable Schwegler wood-concrete

(see Drawing Nos 7, 8, 9, 10, 11, 15, 16, 17, 18 and 19,
pp. 62, 63, 65, 67, 69, 75, 77, 79, 81 and 83, respectively)

 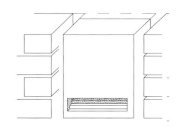

Bat Access Panel 1FE

Can be used to create access or as a roost space by the use of the optional back plate

Access 300 mm (h) x 300 mm (w) x 80 mm (d)

Roost (with back panel) 300 mm (h) x 300 mm (w) x 100 mm (d)

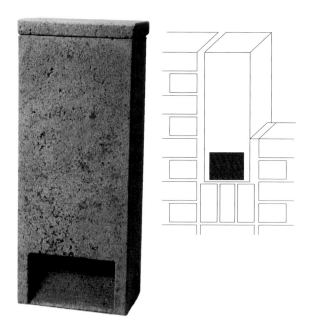

Bat Tube 1FR

Roosting space with wooden roosting panel at rear

475 mm (h) x 200 mm (w) x 125 mm (d)

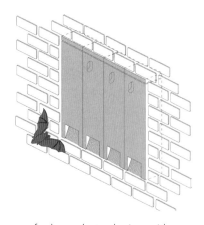

Bat Tube 2FR

For creation of spaces for larger bat colonies, with optional access to other roosting areas from the rear of the product

Dimensions as 1FR, but possible to link as multiple units, as shown above, due to transverse connecting holes

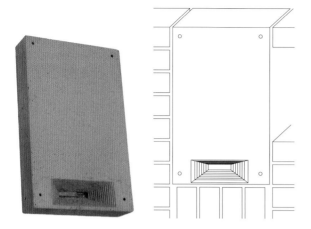

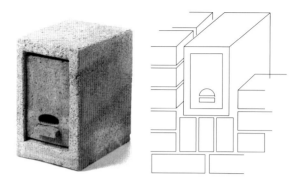

Summer and Winter Batbox 1WI

For installation into the walls of buildings and structures. This design is for hibernation in winter as well as summer use. The interior is designed with different surface textures and areas with changing hanging depths. Uses Schwegler light-concrete

550 mm (h) x 350 mm (w) x 95 mm (d)

Brick Box for Bats Type 27

For installation into the walls of buildings and structures

265 mm (h) x 180 mm (w) x 240 mm (d)

Advantages			Considerations	
Familiar material	N/A		Unfamiliar material; unsure how to protect	✓
Easy to install	Depends on context and surrounding materials		Thermal bridges	Where cavity bridged would need Damp Proof Course (DPC) cavity tray
Durable	✓		Exposed wood particles on cut or damaged edges may absorb moisture	✓
Low or no maintenance	Some access hatches permit internal cleaning		Must be maintained with 'special' unfamiliar paint	Some
Frost resistant	✓		Embodied energy	High
Thermal mass	Medium or high		Embodied carbon	High to medium
Fits UK construction sizes	No		Degree of fit to UK construction sizes	Do not coordinate with UK brick construction in two or three dimensions (see Table 3.2 on dimensions)
			Product uptake	Unknown

Other
- 2FR allows a larger roost area to be provided
- The designs 1FE, 1FR, 2FR and type 27 can either be set flush or can be set into masonry and rendered so that only the entrance is visible
- 1FE and 2FR have the capacity to lead to other roosting areas from the rear of the product
- 1FE is the most versatile of the range and can be incorporated into a number of construction types

Other
- Avoid using aluminium nails
- Non-loadbearing wall will need lintel if used in multiples, side by side

3.3 Bats needing a flying area

These bat species (brown long-eared, grey long-eared and Natterer's) can, in the same way as crevice-dwelling bats, gain access to their roost spaces by crawling through a small gap, but they need a roost in which they can fly especially when females are roosting during the summer. This fact will necessitate the use of a cold roof space in most instances as their need to gain access to a flight area would breach the U value envelope and air-tightness of that part of the structure. Inside the roof space, bats will roost within crevices (see Drawing No. 5), but they will require the additional space for flying and dimensions of 2.8 m (h) x 5 m (w) x 5 m (l) are optimal. It is also important that this space does not have framed or trussed rafters to ensure sufficient flight space. Table 3.7 lists some considerations for these bat species.

Table 3.7: Considerations and key requirements for bats needing flying space

Consideration	Solution
Where in a development	Anywhere where the access is not illuminated by artificial lighting
Where in a building	The crevice roosting provision within the roost is to be located on the south or west side for solar heating. The flight area is not as important
Height	Over 2 m
Roost dimensions	2–2.8 m (h) x 5 m (w) x 5 m (l), not trussed. Ideally 2.8 m height, but a height of 2 m may be acceptable in some circumstances
	To incorporate roost cervices with dimensions of any size as long as some components of the area are crevices in the region of 20–30 mm x width of gap
	Greater total areas of something like 1 sq m would be useful for nursery (summer) roosts
Access dimensions	15–20 mm (h) x 20–50 mm (w)
Other considerations	Rough (for grip)
	Non-toxic and non-corrosive
	No risk of entanglement
	Suitable thermal properties (reducing 24-hour fluctuations), but allowing maximum thermal gain
	Access not lit by artificial lighting

3.4 Horseshoe bats

Horseshoe bats are among the species that have suffered the greatest decline in numbers in recent decades and their range in the UK has also shrunk. Currently their range is restricted predominantly to Wales and south-west England, although it is possible that climate change, along with a hoped for recovery in numbers, could see this range expanding north and east again, assuming suitable foraging habitats and roosting opportunities exist.

Greater and lesser horseshoe bats are both species that need to fly within their roost and, as such, the details of the needs of these bats are largely covered by Section 3.3. However, horseshoe bats have adapted to hang vertically from their roosting places and, as such, have lost the ability to crawl with ease, a capacity common to other bat species. This fact means that, in addition to the needs of bats that require a flying area, horseshoe bats need access through which they can fly, and this must be taken into consideration early on in the design process. Table 3.8 lists some considerations for horseshoe bats.

Table 3.8: Considerations and key requirements for horseshoe bats

Consideration	Solution
Where in a development	Anywhere where the access and flight paths are not illuminated by artificial lighting
Where in a building	The roost is most likely to be in a roof space and this should have an orientation that allows a south-facing solar gain or, better still, an L-shape to allow temperature-range choice
Height	Over 2 m
Dimensions	2–2.8 m (h) x 5 m (w) x 5 m (l), not trussed to allow flight. Ideally 2.8 m height, but a height of 2 m may be acceptable in certain circumstances
Access dimensions	Lesser horseshoes: 300 mm (w) x 200 mm (h) Greater horseshoes: 400 mm (w) x 300 mm (h)
Other considerations	Rough (for grip) Non-toxic and non-corrosive No risk of entanglement Suitable thermal properties (reducing 24-hour fluctuations), but allowing maximum thermal gain Access not lit by artificial lighting

Ideally the access to the roost area should be a simple opening with a canopy above and with the top and bottom of the entrance sloped down and outwards. However, there is a range of considerations and if vandals are likely to be a problem one or two horizontal bars may be added, ensuring that a sufficient gap for flight into the roost is retained. If there is concern about the use of the roof space by less desirable species, such as jackdaws, then Drawing No. 1 (overleaf) shows a design that will prevent their entry as well as protecting against weather. This has been shown to be successful for lesser horseshoe bats in particular.

This drawing (No. 1) illustrates the incorporation of a sloped tunnel that matches the entry gap for the species in question. For greater horseshoes this is 400 mm (w) x 300 mm (h) and for lesser horseshoes it is 300 mm (w) x 200 mm (h). The length of the tunnel with the overshot top section prevents the entry of rain, while the steepness of the tunnel (with the lower surface being smooth) prevents jackdaws, pigeons, etc., from either flying or scrabbling their way in. The access should be positioned so that the bats can fly into cover nearby. As with all bat access, it should not be illuminated by artificial light (see Section 4.1).

For greater horseshoe bats there is some evidence that these measures to prevent the entry of other species could detract from the likelihood of the use of the roost by this species. Other alternative measures, such as an internal 'hopper', could be used and further details for consideration can be found in the Vincent Wildlife Trust publication *The Lesser Horseshoe Bat* (Schofield, 2008; www.vwt.org.uk) and the *Natural England Bat Mitigation Guidelines* (Mitchell-Jones, 2004; www.naturalengland.org.uk). It is recommended that the advice of an experienced ecologist is utilised to discuss the best option.

While the other bat species that need a flying space also need to have somewhere within the roost where they can access a more enclosed area, for horseshoe bats this does not apply. What is important is the roughness of the surfaces from which the bats can hang. While it is often surprising to

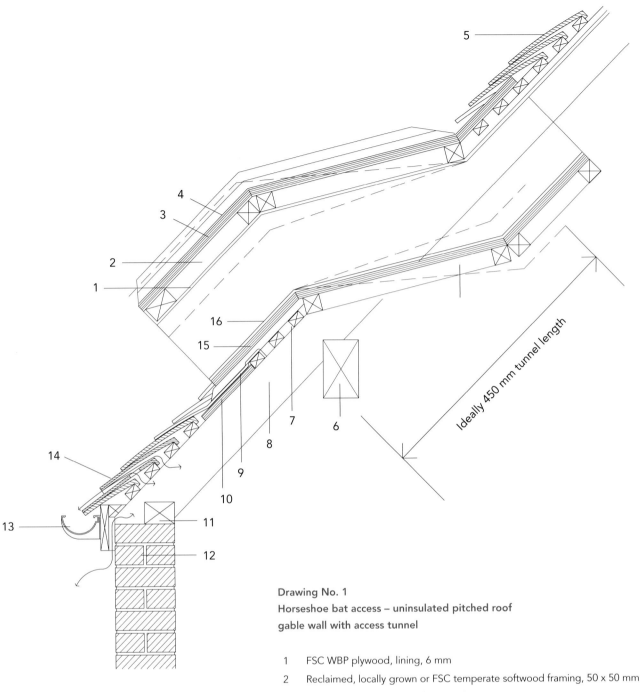

Drawing No. 1

Horseshoe bat access – uninsulated pitched roof gable wall with access tunnel

1   FSC WBP plywood, lining, 6 mm

2   Reclaimed, locally grown or FSC temperate softwood framing, 50 x 50 mm

3   FSC WBP Water Boil Proof plywood, 25 mm

4   Malleable metal standing seam roof cladding

5   Clay plain tile roofing

6   Reclaimed, locally grown or FSC temperate durable hardwood

7   Reclaimed, locally grown or FSC temperate softwood roofing battens

8   Reclaimed, locally grown or FSC temperate softwood rafters

9   Malleable metal apron flashing

10 FSC WBP water boil proof plywood, 25 mm

11 Reclaimed, locally grown or FSC temperate durable hardwood

12 Clay brick solid wall, 1B, 215 mm

13 'Lindab Rainline' Rainwater gutter (Galvanized steel, half round)

14 Bat access tile set, 18 mm gap x 165 mm long

15 FSC WBP water boil proof plywood, 25 mm

16 Anti-bird slope slip plain, Perspex, 6 mm

see horseshoe bats clinging to surfaces that appear to give little purchase, if the surface is very smooth, like some roofing membranes can be, then suitable netting or some rough timber would need to be added.

3.5 Swifts

In order to breed, swifts need access to a space that is fairly flat in buildings where they can construct their simple nest. As swifts like to nest within a space or cavity, their presence as a nesting bird is not generally visible. It is therefore important to ensure that anyone involved in the future maintenance of the building is aware of their use of the building. Table 3.9 lists some considerations for swifts.

Extensive information about swifts and, in particular, about how to design and site swift boxes can be found at the Swift Conservation website (www.swift-conservation.org).

Table 3.9: Considerations and key requirements for swifts

Consideration	Solution
Where in a development	Anywhere high, shaded and free from disturbance and obstructions to their flight paths
Where in a building	Out of direct sunlight, such as under deep eaves or an aspect of the building that does not receive much direct sunlight
	Not adjacent to climbing plants that may give predators, such as rodents, access to the nest
	Where the swifts will have clear airspace into which they can fly from their nests
	Preferably integral to the building, but where this is not possible, external under the eaves, under roof edges and gables
	It is important to have several potential nest sites for swifts in one area
Height	At least 5 m
Dimensions	400 mm (w) x 200 mm (d) x 150 mm (h) ideally, but can be slightly smaller
Access dimensions	30 mm (h) x 65 mm (w) oval or rectangle
Other considerations	Swifts are colonial nesters so, where room allows, it is preferable to have more than one swift nest incorporated into a building. As a guide:
	1 to 4 nest provisions on a house
	4 to 10 on a small block of flats
	10 to 20 on a larger building, e.g. offices or industrial site
	In establishing a new colony, playing recorded swift calls is advised to bring birds in to find the nest places

Ibstock Swift Box
Ibstock

TYPE OF PRODUCT: Swift box

WEBSITE: www.Ibstock.com

WHERE USED: Discrete nesting box for location near eaves. Replaces two whole and two half bricks in single leaf of cavity wall construction

PRODUCT INFORMATION: Available in smooth red and smooth blue

Dimensions: 140 mm (h) x 326 mm (w) x 102 mm (d)

PRODUCT USE: Swift nesting – ensure it is fitted with the entrance hole towards the bottom edge of the front panel

Nest contained within product

(see Drawing No. 8, p. 63)

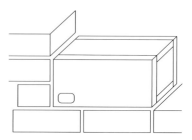

Advantages			Considerations			
Familiar material	✓		Unfamiliar material; unsure how to protect	N/A		
Easy to install	✓		Thermal bridges	N/A		
Durable	Outer face		Exposed wood particles on cut or damaged edges may absorb moisture	N/A		
Low or no maintenance	Outer face		Must be maintained with 'special' unfamiliar paint	N/A		
Frost resistant	✓		Embodied energy	Medium		
Thermal mass	Medium or high		Embodied carbon	Depends on fuel used		
Fits UK construction sizes	✓		Degree of fit to UK construction sizes	✓ ✓ ✓ (fits all 3 dimensions)		
			Product uptake	Unknown		

Other
- Could be used in multiple arrangements with mortared purpend between (but lintel required)
- Fairfaced, no need for rendering

Other

Swift and Bat Box 1MF
Schwegler GmbH

TYPE OF PRODUCT: Swift and bat box

WEBSITE: www.schwegler-nature.com

WHERE USED: The box is hung from a galvanized mild-steel mounting plate

Using the Bat Slope, the 1MF can be built directly into the brickwork of a wall, with the box flush with the face of the wall and access to the rear space for bats

PRODUCT INFORMATION: Schwegler wood-concrete

1MF with Bat Slope:
700 mm (h) x 430 mm (w) x 225 mm (d)

Bat Slope:
250 mm (h) x 430 mm (w) x 225 mm (d)

Combined height: 700 mm

PRODUCT USE: The 1MF contains two nesting chambers for swifts, each with its own entrance. A recess in the rear panel creates a space between the wall of the building and box for use by bats

(see Drawing Nos 12, 13 and 14, pp. 70, 71 and 73, respectively)

Without bat slope   With bat slope

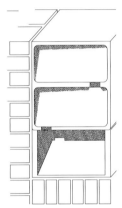

Advantages			Considerations			
Familiar material	N/A		Unfamiliar material; unsure how to protect	✓		
Easy to install	Depends on context and surrounding materials		Thermal bridges	Where cavities are bridged will need damp proof course (DPC) cavity tray		
Durable	✓		Exposed wood particles on cut or damaged edges may absorb moisture	✓		
Low or no maintenance	Access hatches permit internal cleaning		Must be maintained with 'special' unfamiliar paint	Some		
Frost resistant	✓		Embodied energy	High		
Thermal mass	Medium or high		Embodied carbon	High to medium		
Fits UK construction sizes	No		Degree of fit to UK construction sizes	Not good in 3 dimensions		
			Product uptake	Unknown		
Other			Other			

Other
- Reduces U value if bridging cavity
- Thicker walls needed to accommodate
- Avoid using aluminium nails

Swift Box Type 25
Schwegler GmbH

TYPE OF PRODUCT: Swift box

WEBSITE: www.schwegler-nature.com

WHERE USED: For installation into walls of buildings and structures

PRODUCT INFORMATION: Schwegler wood-concrete

180 mm (h) x 265 mm (w) x 220 mm (d)

Entrance hole: 33 mm (h) x 55 mm (w)

PRODUCT USE: Swift nesting

 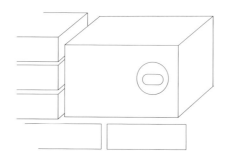

Advantages		Considerations	
Familiar material	N/A	Unfamiliar material; unsure how to protect	✓
Easy to install	Depends on context and surrounding materials	Thermal bridges	Where cavity walls bridged will need DPC cavity tray
Durable	✓	Exposed wood particles on cut or damaged edges may absorb moisture	✓
Low or no maintenance	No access hatches to permit internal cleaning	Must be maintained with 'special' unfamiliar paint	N/A
Frost resistant	✓	Embodied energy	High
Thermal mass	Medium or high	Embodied carbon	High to medium
Fits UK construction sizes	No	Degree of fit to UK construction sizes	Not good in 3 dimensions
		Product uptake	Unknown
Other		Other	
		• Reduces U value if bridging cavity	
		• Thicker walls needed to accommodate	
		• Avoid using aluminium nails	

Swift Box Type 16
Schwegler GmbH

TYPE OF PRODUCT: Swift box

WEBSITE: www.schwegler-nature.com

WHERE USED: For installation into the walls of buildings and structures

PRODUCT INFORMATION: Schwegler wood-concrete

240 mm (h) x 430 mm (w) x 220 mm (d)

PRODUCT USE: Swift nesting

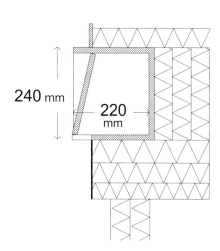

Advantages			Considerations		
Familiar material	N/A		Unfamiliar material; unsure how to protect	✓	
Easy to install	Depends on context and surrounding materials		Thermal bridges	Where cavities walls bridged	
Durable	✓		Exposed wood particles on cut or damaged edges may absorb moisture	✓	
Low or no maintenance	Some – no access hatches to permit internal cleaning		Must be maintained with 'special' unfamiliar paint	N/A	
Frost resistant	✓		Embodied energy	High	
Thermal mass	Medium or high		Embodied carbon	High to medium	
Fits UK construction sizes	No		Degree of fit to UK construction sizes	Not good in 3 dimensions	
			Product uptake	There has been some success recorded with this swift box	
Other			Other		

Other (Considerations):
- Reduces U value if bridging cavity
- Thicker walls needed to accommodate
- Avoid using aluminium nails
- Will need DPC tray across cavity

3.6 Swallows

When swallows construct their nests they use around 1,000 pellets of mud taken from the edges of ponds, puddles and rivers. The nest is built by both sexes, and they mate for life. Suitable ledges or ready-made nests can be provided. Table 3.10 lists some considerations for swallows.

Table 3.10: Considerations and key requirements for swallows

Consideration	Solution
Where in a development	Inside a cold roof space or other unheated structure not requiring thermal insulation nor included in air-tightness testing, such as garages and outbuildings. Possibly under very deep eaves
Where in a building	Swallows prefer to nest inside outbuildings which provide dark ledges and nooks and crannies for nesting. These are protected from the worst of the cold weather and remain cool when it is hot. There needs to be permanent access
Height	It needs to be out of the reach of predators, such as cats
Dimensions	Fix a nest platform or ready-made nest where it would be suitable for them to nest. This needs to be 260 mm (w) x 100 mm (d)
Access dimensions	Minimum 50 mm (h) and 70 mm (w)
Other considerations	Droppings will occur below the nest, so locate the nest wisely or provide a ledge to catch the droppings The nesting area only needs to receive a minimal amount of daylight

Swallows

3.7 House martins

Various ready-made house martin nests are available. They do not guarantee that martins will nest, but often encourage them to build their own. As well as ready-made nests, it is possible to make nests that mimic these from exterior fillers or a mixture of cement and sawdust. These should measure about 180 mm in diameter, with a semi-circular entrance hole measuring 25 mm high and 60–65 mm wide. The nest can be mounted on a board or fixed directly to the building. Table 3.11 lists some considerations for house martins.

Table 3.11: Considerations and key requirements for house martins

Consideration	Solution
Where in a development	External under overhanging eaves with unobstructed access
Where on a building	These are usually mounted on a board and can be fixed easily under the eaves. Nests are best placed in groups and there is some evidence that martins prefer to nest on north- and east-facing walls
Height	At least 5 m
Dimensions	180 mm in diameter
Access dimensions	A semi-circular hole 25 mm high and 60–65 mm wide
Other considerations	Ensure that the nest is under an overhang to protect it from the weather Nests can be fixed in groups to increase the likelihood of use Place nests away from areas where droppings may be a nuisance

House martins' ready-made nest

3.8 House sparrows

Pairs are faithful to their nest site and to each other for life, although a lost mate of either sex is normally replaced within days. Sparrows prefer to nest in holes in an occupied building, but they regularly use other kinds of holes, for example in trees, and nest boxes. Table 3.12 lists some considerations for house sparrows.

Table 3.12: Considerations and key requirements for house sparrows

Consideration	Solution
Where in a development	Any suitable building
Where in a building	Ideally within the structure at the soffit/eaves level, but otherwise as an external box at the same location Out of direct sunlight – the preferred aspect is easterly
Height	At least 2 m
Dimensions	350 mm (h) x 150 mm (w) x 150 mm (d)
Access dimensions	A 32 mm round hole
Other considerations	House sparrows nest in loose colonies of 10–20 pairs. Since they do not defend a territory, nests can be as little as 20–30 cm apart

Brick Box Type 24
Schwegler GmbH

TYPE OF PRODUCT:	House sparrow brick box
WEBSITE:	www.schwegler-nature.com
WHERE USED:	For incorporation into an outer wall as appropriate
PRODUCT INFORMATION:	Made of woodcrete
	Dimensions: 235 mm (h) x 180 mm (w) x 180 mm (d)
	Entrance hole 32 mm
	The brick boxes can be installed flush with the outside wall and can be rendered or covered so that only the entrance hole is visible
PRODUCT USE:	As well as sparrows, the box may also be used by great, blue and coal tits, redstart and nuthatch

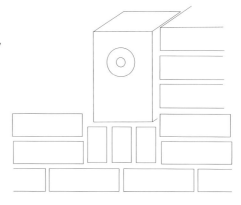

Advantages			Considerations		
Familiar material	N/A		Unfamiliar material; unsure how to protect	✓	
Easy to install	Depends on context and surrounding materials and sizes		Thermal bridges	Where cavities walls bridged will need DPC cavity tray	
Durable	✓		Exposed wood particles on cut or damaged edges may absorb moisture	✓	
Low or no maintenance	Some – access hatches permit internal cleaning		Must be maintained with 'special' unfamiliar paint	N/A	
Frost resistant	✓		Embodied energy	High	
Thermal mass	Medium or high		Embodied carbon	High to medium	
Fits UK construction sizes	No		Degree of fit to UK construction sizes	Poor in 3 dimensions	
			Product uptake	Unknown	
Other			Other		
			• Reduces U value if bridging cavity wall		
			• Thicker walls needed to accommodate		
			• Avoid using aluminium nails		

Sparrow Terrace 1SP
Schwegler GmbH

TYPE OF PRODUCT: House sparrow multiple nest

WEBSITE: www.schwegler-nature.com

RENDERED SURFACE: Installation and additional insulation layer (2–4 cm), if necessary

WHERE USED: For incorporation into an outer wall as appropriate

PRODUCT INFORMATION: Made of woodcrete

240 mm (h) x 430 mm (w) x 220 mm (d)

Complete installation as a nesting block within brick or concrete walls. To avoid conducting low temperatures, also use wall insulation or install at a suitable depth in the wall (manufacturer's recommendation)

PRODUCT USE: For use in all types of built structures

 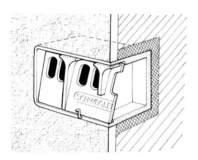

Advantages			Considerations		
Familiar material	N/A		Unfamiliar material; unsure how to protect	✓	
Easy to install	Depends on context and surrounding materials and sizes		Thermal bridges	Major thermal bridge where cavity wall bridged will need DPC cavity tray	
Durable	✓		Exposed wood particles on cut or damaged edges may absorb moisture	✓	
Low or no maintenance	No access hatches to permit internal cleaning		Must be maintained with 'special' unfamiliar paint	N/A	
Frost resistant	✓		Embodied energy	High	
Thermal mass	Medium or high		Embodied carbon	High to medium	
Fits UK construction sizes	No		Degree of fit to UK construction sizes	Poor in 3 dimensions	
			Product uptake	Unknown	
Other			Other		
			• Thicker walls needed to accommodate • Avoid using aluminium nails		

RoofBLOCK
RoofBLOCK

TYPE OF PRODUCT: Bird block – concrete eaves/verge system

WEBSITE: www.roofblock.co.uk

WHERE USED: Flat, hipped or any pitch roof. Outer leaf of cavity wall or half brick extension of solid wall

PRODUCT INFORMATION: Made from recycled aggregates and eco-cement

PRODUCT USE: Block with 30 mm hole to allow access to hollow section of product

(see Drawing Nos 2 and 6, pp. 54 and 61)

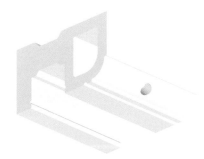

Advantages		Considerations	
Familiar material	✓	Unfamiliar material; unsure how to protect	N/A
Easy to install	Must be designed in	Thermal bridges	Risk of thermal bridge through thin cavity wall construction – can be improved with wider insulated cavity (see below)
Durable	✓	Exposed wood particles on cut or damaged edges may absorb moisture	N/A
Low or no maintenance	✓	Must be maintained with 'special' unfamiliar paint	N/A
Frost resistant	✓	Embodied energy	Medium
Thermal mass	High	Embodied carbon	Low (EcoCement)
Fits UK construction sizes	✓	Degree of fit to UK construction sizes	✓ ✓ (see Table 3.2)
		Product uptake	Unknown

Other
- Numerous endorsements and accolades
- Can be positioned on any elevation unobtrusively
- Made for cavity walls, but will fit on half brick extension of 1B solid wall
- Fairfaced, no need for rendering over

Other
- Reduces U value locally in wider cavity wall construction with full fill cavity insulation
- Profile may need to be modified to suit thicker walls and thicker insulation (see Drawing No. 6)
- Eco-cement should have less embodied carbon
- Recycled aggregates are likely to have less embodied energy and/or carbon

3.9 Starlings

Starlings nest in holes and cavities, especially in trees, but often use holes in buildings, including occupied houses and nest boxes. They nest in loose colonies and do not establish and defend a territory – only the immediate area around the nesting cavity is defended. The whole colony feeds communally in what is termed a home range.

In order to attract a mate, the male builds the base of the nest from dry grass and leaves in a hole, and sings from perches close to the nest's entrance. The female completes the nest by forming the inner cup shape of the nest and lining it with fine grasses, moss and feathers. No ready-made nest boxes for use in built structures exist, but the dimensions can be used to incorporate a bespoke space. Table 3.13 lists some considerations for starlings.

Table 3.13: Considerations and key requirements for starlings

Consideration	Solution
Where in a development	Any suitable building
Where in a building	Ideally within the structure at the soffit/eaves level, but otherwise as an external box at the same location
	Out of direct sunlight – the preferred aspect is easterly – and not over the main living areas as starlings can be noisy
Height	At least 3 m high
Dimensions	400 mm (h) x 180 mm (w) x 180 mm (d)
Access dimensions	45 mm round hole – this hole needs to be located at least 125 mm above the base of the box
Other considerations	Nest provision should be several metres apart

3.10 Barn owls

Although barn owls are not an urban species, any suitable new buildings in a development that are on the edge of a built-up area could play host to a barn owl. Table 3.14 gives details to be used when considering the potential for the provision of barn owls and their key requirements.

Drawing Nos 2 and 3 illustrate the incorporation of this access into a roof space. This is shown as being via the gable end wall and also via the roof itself. Within the roof space a nest box can be provided and details of these are found on the Barn Owl Trust website (www.barnowltrust.org.uk).

It is possible that the provision for barn owls could also be utilised by the little owl. This owl was introduced into Britain during the nineteenth century and is found in low numbers across much of England and parts of Wales. In order to make provision specific for little owls, information can be found on the Barn Owl Trust website (www.barnowltrust.org.uk).

Table 3.14: Considerations and key requirements for barn owls

Consideration	Solution
Type of location	The surrounding habitat needs to be open countryside (not urban or woodland) – as a general rule of thumb, no provision should be made within 1 km of a major road (dual-carriageway or motorway) or at over 300 m above sea level
Where in a development	A suitable building would be one on the edge of the development, ideally with the access point facing open countryside One of the tallest buildings should normally be selected
Where in a building	Their requirements mean that provision for barn owls is most straightforward in buildings that have a cold roof space and for which there is not likely to be a planned conversion into a used area that would incorporate the nesting area However, it is possible to dedicate only part of a roof space to the owls, so long as a separation ensures that the owls will be hidden from view should the other part of the roof be used Alternatively, in bespoke cases, the U value envelope can be diverted to incorporate a nesting area of the dimensions given below within an exterior wall. This will need additional measures to maintain the U value envelope and early consultation between the architect and the Barn Owl Trust is recommended
Height	Access hole and nesting area no less than 3 m above ground level
Dimensions	Floor area of a nest chamber: absolute minimum 400 mm x 400 mm, ideal size is 1 sq m Minimum height: 600 mm Minimum drop from bottom of entrance hole to floor: 460 mm
Access dimensions	Access need not be by flight, but walking Entrance hole: minimum size 100 mm (w) x 200 mm (h); optimum size 130 mm (w) x 250 mm (h); maximum size 200 mm (w) x 300 mm (h) Measures aimed at reducing the chances of entry by other species (such as jackdaws) are recommended, provided that they do not significantly reduce the box's suitability for barn owls Hipped roofs, and pitched roofs where optimal siting of the access is through the roof rather than the wall/gable end, will require the use of a specially built miniature dormer or owl-hole 'tile' – see Drawing No. 3 Where the access is in a vertical structure, such as a wall or gable end, there should be an external landing platform or perch below the entrance hole to facilitate the barn owl's arrival and departure (see Drawing No. 2)
Other considerations	Barn owls seem to prefer perching on wood, rather than metal or stone (presumably for comfort and minimum heat loss) Human access for easy clearing-out of pellet debris (very occasionally) is essential Barn owls can easily become accustomed to almost any type of regular human activity or noise

Further advice and information can be obtained in the Barn Owl Trust/ Natural England publication *Barn Owls and Rural Planning Applications 'What needs to happen': A Guide for Planners*, which includes an appendix entitled 'Making provision for barn owls, a guide for planners, applicants and developers', and also via the Barn Owl Trust website (www.barnowltrust.org.uk).

Barn owls' entrance in wall

Drawing No. 2
Barn owl wall entrance – uninsulated pitched roof gable wall
(above insulated wall)

1 Reclaimed, locally grown or FSC temperate softwood roofing battens
2 Reclaimed, locally grown or FSC temperate softwood rafters
3 Extruded cellular fired clay tunnel to cross cavity with landing and take-off areas outside of wall thickness
3a Eco-concrete tunnel to cross cavity with landing and take-off areas outside of wall thickness
3b Precast concrete tunnel to cross cavity
4 Un-insulated cavity above occupied floors
5 Concrete block inner leaf, 100 mm
6 Support brackets, Galvanized Mild Steel or Austenitic Stainless Steel
7 DIY Swift Box, using cement and wood fibre board, 25 mm.
 Size: 180 (h) x 220 (d) x 265 (w) mm
8 'Ibstock bat brick' 2 No. brick size, bottom to bottom to form larger opening
9 Fired clay facing brick outer leaf, 102 x 215 x 65 mm
10 'Ibstock bat brick' 3 No. to form sides and top of opening, brick size
11 Metal tie for tunnel, Stainless steel
12 'RoofBLOCK masonry roof overhang system' Hollow precast eco-concrete verge system incorporating bat or bird roosts
13 Clay plain tile roofing
14 Option: 2 part long wall tie, austenitic stainless steel (304 equivalent), 400 mm
14a Option: 'MagmaTech TeploTie Type 4', extruded basalt and fibre long wall tie, 425 x 6.5 dia. mm
15 Cavity tray DPC damp proof course (stepped)
16 'Pro clima Solitex Plus' WTL Wind Tightness Layer and VPU vapour permeable underlay

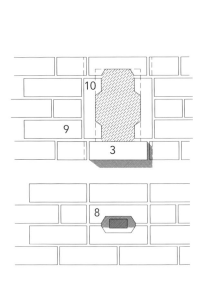

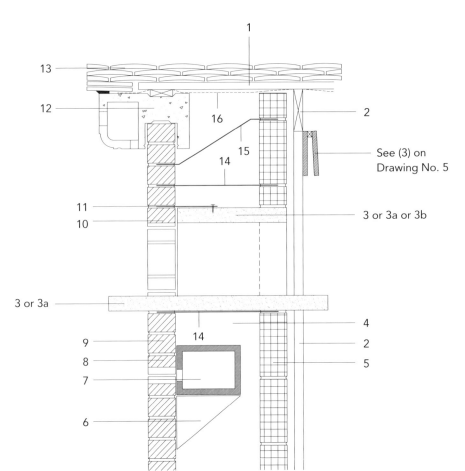

Drawing No. 3
Barn owl roof entrance – uninsulated hip or pitched roof dormer (above insulated wall)

1   Reclaimed, locally grown or FSC temperate durable hardwood frame, 38 mm x 38 mm – 50 mm x 50 mm softwood edges

2   FSC WBP water boil proof plywood, 25 mm

3   Reclaimed, locally grown or FSC temperate softwood framing, 50 mm x 50 mm

4   FSC WBP water boil proof plywood, 25 mm

5   Malleable metal standing seam roof cladding

6   Reclaimed, locally grown or FSC temperate softwood roof tiling battens

7   Clay plain tile roofing

8   Reclaimed, locally grown or FSC temperate softwood rafters

9   Drain hole in (11)

10 Reclaimed, locally grown or FSC temperate durable hardwood purlin

11 FSC WBP water boil proof plywood, 25 mm, installed to fall to drain hole (9)

12 Malleable metal apron flashing

13 FSC WBP water boil proof plywood, 25 mm

14 Reclaimed, locally grown or FSC temperate durable hardwood wall plate

15 Clay brick solid wall, 1B, 215 mm

16 Lindab Rainline Rainwater gutter (galvanized steel, half round)

17 Bat access tile set, 18 mm gap x 165 mm long

Barn owls' entrance in sloping roof

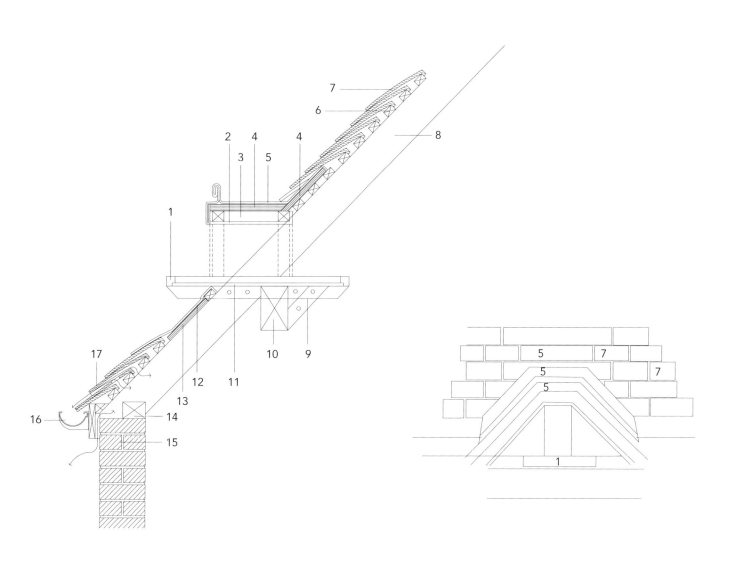

3.11 Peregrine falcons

The nest site, known as an eyrie, is usually on a cliff ledge, quarry or other inaccessible and undisturbed location, although buildings and other constructions are increasingly being used. Old nests of other species, such as ravens, are used elsewhere in the world, but rarely in the UK. The nest itself is a slight scrape in any earth or old debris on the nest ledge. No material is brought in to build a nest. Table 3.15 lists some considerations for peregrine falcons.

Table 3.15: Considerations and key requirements for peregrine falcons

Consideration	Solution
Where in a development	On a wide ledge, free from disturbance and as high as possible
Where on a building	Avoid full sun and prevailing winds North or north-east preferable
Height	Over 20 m
Dimensions	Ledge: 40 mm (h) x 600 mm (w) 450 mm (d) Box: 900 mm (h) x 600 mm (w) x 450 mm (d) (see www.raptorresource.org/build.htm or ready-made Schwegler products)
Access dimensions	N/A for ledge
Other considerations	Place the provision where routine maintenance is least likely to disturb peregrines using the ledge Place the provision where the discarded remains of prey and pellets will not inconvenience the users of the building Peregrines are vocal when on the nest so consider the location of the provision with this in mind

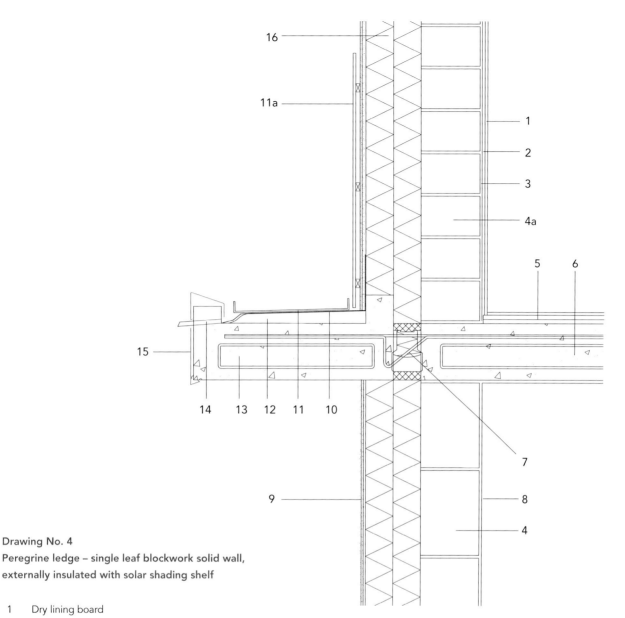

Drawing No. 4
Peregrine ledge – single leaf blockwork solid wall,
externally insulated with solar shading shelf

1   Dry lining board

2   'Dot and dab' bonded drylining

3   Airtight parge coat: clay, lime or gypsum, 5-8 mm or plaster

4   Dense aggregate concrete block 140 mm x 215 mm x 440 mm

4a 140 mm block laid on side, 150 mm course height, 215 mm thick wall

5   'Dry Screed' boards: dense desulfurisation gypsum with wood fibre reinforcement

6   Insitu reinforced concrete floor, 200 mm

7   'Schöck Isokorb Type K' thermal break with intumescent fire protection and
    continuity reinforcement

8   Gypsum plaster finish

9   Lime, hemp-lime or mineral based thin render system 2 layers, reinforcement layer
    between (airtight and permeable) (not cement based)

10 Waterproof membrane with upstand

11 Stainless steel tray, 450 x 600 x 40 mm

11a Wall protection upstand 900 mm

12 Sand:cement screed to 1:40 fall

13 Cantilever shelf, insitu concrete, 200 mm

14 Drain spout

15 Pressed metal fascia/coping/drip

16 Dense thermal insulation, 2 x 100 mm

3.12 Bespoke roost and nesting provision in low and zero carbon building types

Having reviewed each species, the products that can be bought ready-made for some of these and how they relate to standard building dimensions, consideration is now given to how they can be incorporated into a new build. This section discusses each of the major sorts of new build likely to be most widely used in low and zero carbon buildings and the opportunities for provision that arise in each.

It is important to note that where a ready-made product is shown as an example, other products with suitable dimensions or bespoke designs can be made to utilise the available space.

All of the suggestions made are based on what is known of the requirements of the species in question and finding ways to incorporate these into each build style, without compromising the integrity of the building and its compliance with energy standards. The success of these measures cannot be guaranteed, but any resultant monitoring of uptake will aid our development and understanding to help ensure increasing success in the future.

3.12.1 Roof space

Drawing Nos 5 and 6 provide provision for crevice-dwelling bats in a roof design that uses tiles and allows access to the space between the tiles/slates and the U value envelope. Included in these figures are examples of the placement of some of the ready-made products, as well as bespoke bat-roosting areas.

Drawing No. 5
Roofspace 1 – solid wall construction at roof eaves and ridge providing places for bats and birds (uninsulated outbuilding)

1	Ridge roost, similar materials to (3c)
1a	Option: Could be empty ridge tile space with closed ends and ways through to next ridge tile space
2	Handmade clay ridge tile with bat access
3	Bat roost fixed to side of rafters below ridge beam, 2 boards spaced apart, 15–20 mm minimum, 25–30 mm maximum
3a	Option: Reclaimed, locally grown or FSC temperate softwood scraps
3b	Option: FSC WBP water boil proof plywood strips
3c	Option: Cement-wood particle board, Roughened/grooved surface for climbing and hanging
4	Reclaimed, locally grown or FSC temperate softwood rafters, 200 mm (avoid trussed rafters)
5	Reclaimed, locally grown or FSC temperate durable hardwood wall plate
6	As (7)
7	Potential roost/nest box/platform positions (not necessarily all together, along length of building) some face fixed, some sheltering under others
8	Bat access tile set, 18 mm gap x 165 mm long
9	Handmade clay plain tile roofing, 265 mm x 160 mm x 10 mm
10	Mortar bedding
11	Reclaimed, locally grown or FSC Oak or durable hardwood ridge purlin

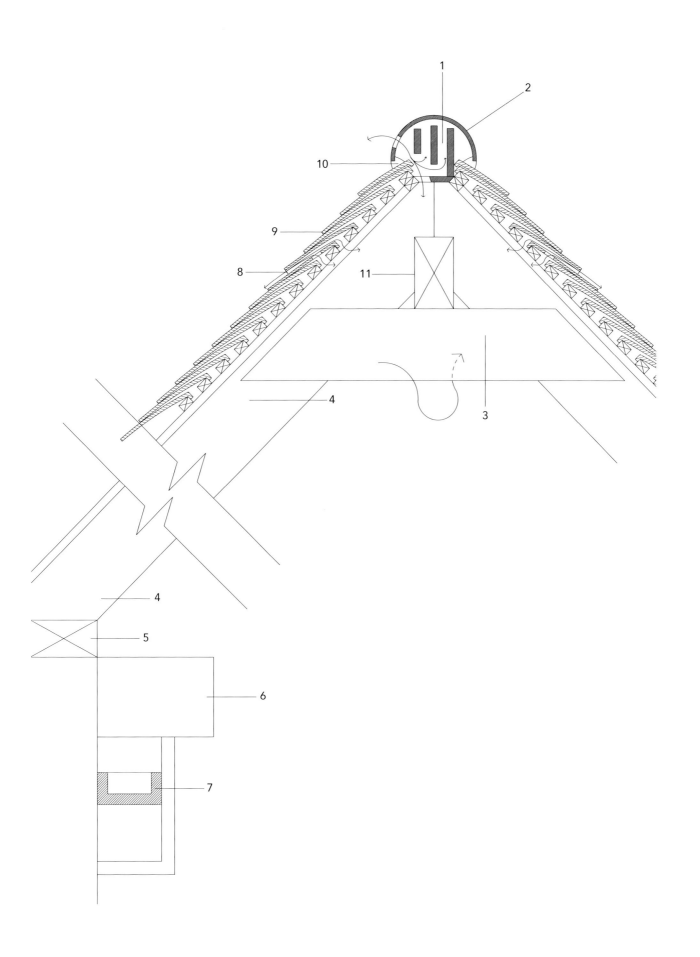

Drawing No. 6
Roofspace 2 – Insulated cavity wall and pitched roof
providing places for bats and small birds

1 Additional layer of underlay below gap supported on FSC board on battens

2 'Pro clima Intello Plus' ATL Air tightness layer, polyolefine, lapped and sealed joints

3 Cellulose fibre insulation, 3 x 100 mm

4 Drylining ceiling board

5 Reclaimed, locally grown or FSC temperate softwood wall plate, 75 x 100 mm with GMS holding down straps

6 Air tight parge coat: clay, lime or gypsum, 5–8 mm or plaster

7 Cellular clay blockwork inner leaf, 100 mm

8 Reclaimed, locally grown or FSC temperate softwood wall plate, 100 x 75 mm

9 Full fill cavity wall insulation, 3 x 100 mm rock mineral fibre

10 Option: 2 part long wall tie, austenitic stainless steel (304 equivalent), 400 mm

10a Option: 'MagmaTech TeploTie Type 4', extruded basalt and fibre long wall tie, 425 x 6.5 dia. mm

11 Fired clay facing brick outer leaf, 102 x 215 x 65 mm

12 'RoofBLOCK masonry roof overhang system' Hollow precast 'eco-concrete' eaves/verge system incorporating bird or bat roosts (modified size required and shown here)

13 Gutter galvanized mild steel (half round)

14 Reclaimed, locally grown or FSC temperate softwood rafters, 200 mm (avoid trussed rafters)

15 Bat access tile set, 18 mm gap x 165 long mm

16 Cement-wood particle board, Roughened/grooved surface for climbing and hanging

17 'Pro clima Solitex Plus' WTL Wind Tightness Layer vapour permeable roofing underlay (breathing roof), lapped and sealed joints

17a Gap in underlay (17) below bat access tile set (15)

18 Reclaimed, locally grown or FSC temperate durable species softwood roof tiling battens

19 Handmade clay plain tile roofing, 265 x 160 x 10 mm

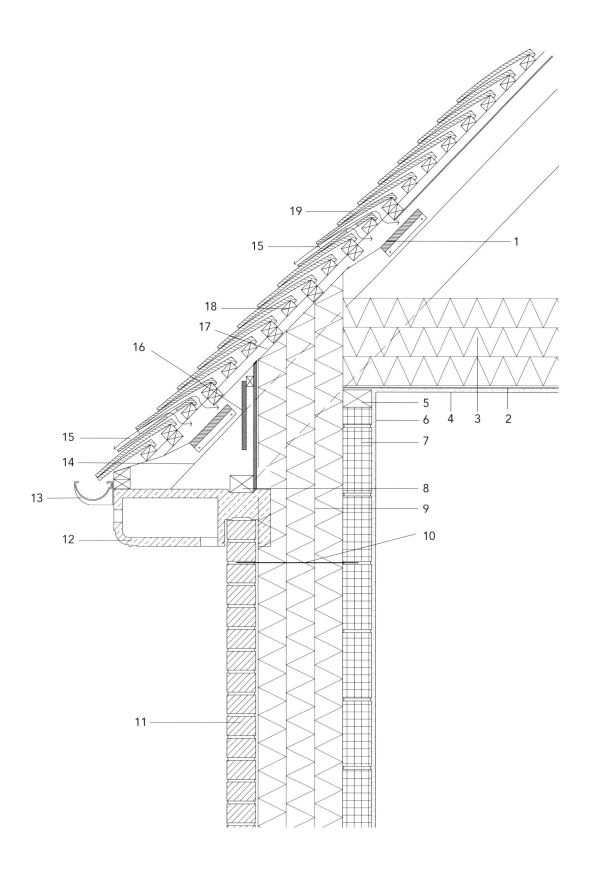

3.12.2 Cavity walls

Unfilled cavity walls in traditional build styles are used by a number of bat species. The term cavity wall is used here to denote insulated cavity walls that, despite their seemingly inappropriate build style for low and zero carbon buildings, are nevertheless anticipated to continue to be built for some considerable time and do provide opportunities for bat roosting and bird nesting.

Drawing Nos 7 to 11 show ready-made products for bats and swifts (the Ibstock Enclosed Bat Box (see p. 33), the Ibstock Swift Box (see p. 42), Tudor Bat Access Tile Set (see p. 30) and the Schweglar Bat Roost 1FE (see p. 36)) as well as the bespoke provision of space for crevice bat roosting in a variety of options.

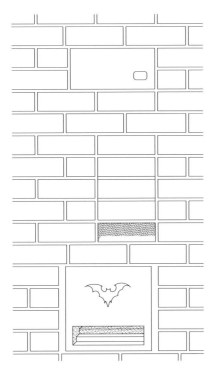

Drawing No. 7
Cavity walls 1

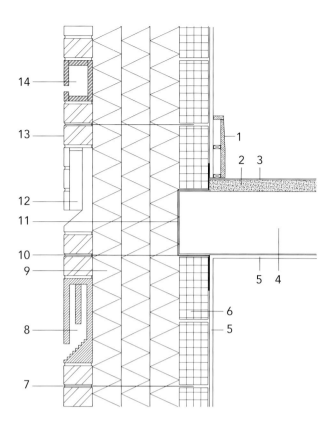

Drawing No. 8
Cavity walls 2 – brick/block cavity wall construction providing spaces for bats

1   Hollow skirting board (and dado rails) carrying services to avoid chasing masonry walls

2   'Eco-screed': Less OP cement and more GGBS ground granulated burst furnace slag cement, less virgin aggregate and more recycled, secondary or manufactured aggregate, 40 mm

3   Linoleum sheet flooring, 2 mm

4   Precast concrete hollow plank floor, see (11)

5   In-situ plaster for airtightness: clay, lime or gypsum

6   Locally manufactured dense recycled aggregate concrete block with lime mortar

7   2 part long wall tie, austenitic stainless steel (304 equivalent), 400 mm

8   'Schwegler Bat Box 1FE 00748/3', wood-concrete, 300 x 300 x 100 mm. Best located at eaves level not at lower levels

8a Option: DIY Bat Box using cement and wood fibre board, grooved surface for climbing and hanging, 25 mm. Best located at eaves level not at lower levels (not shown on plan)

9   Rock mineral fibre full fill cavity wall batts, 3 x 100 mm

10 MagmaTech TeploTie Type 4', extruded basalt and fibre long wall tie, 425 x 6.5 dia. mm

11 'Pro clima Solitex Plus' WTL Wind Tightness Layer: Top hat profile closing ends of hollow core plank floor, see (4)

12 'Ibstock Bat Box' 215 x 290 x 102 mm. Best located at eaves level not at lower levels

13 Reclaimed or new locally sourced facing brick, 102 x 215 x 65 mm lime mortar

14 'Ibstock Swift Box' 326 x 140 x 102 mm. Best located at eaves level not at lower levels

Drawing No. 9
Cavity walls 3
(top) Brick/block cavity wall construction (non-breathing roof, ventilated eaves)
(bottom) Brick/block cavity gable wall construction verge providing spaces for bats and swifts

1	Hemp insulation, 3 x 100 mm
2	Drylining ceiling board
3	Reclaimed, locally grown or FSC temperate softwood wall plate, 75 x 100 mm with holding down straps
4	Cellular blockwork inner leaf, 100 mm
5	Airtight parge coat: clay, lime or gypsum, 5–8 mm or plaster
6	Full fill cavity wall insulation, 3 x 100 mm rock mineral fibre
7	Wall ties option: 2 part long wall tie, austenitic stainless steel (304 equivalent), 400 mm
7a	Wall ties option: 'MagmaTech TeploTie Type 4', extruded basalt and fibre long wall tie, 425 x 6.5 dia. mm
8	Reclaimed, locally made fired clay facing brick outer leaf, 102 x 215 x 65 mm
9	Reclaimed, locally grown or FSC temperate durable species softwood soffit
10	Reclaimed, locally grown or FSC temperate durable species softwood fascia
11	Gutter and brackets, galvanized steel, half round
12	Rigid HDPE flashing into gutter
13	Reclaimed, locally grown or FSC temperate softwood tilting fillet, 50 mm x varies
14	'Bat access tile-set', 18 mm gap x 165 mm long, gap in underlay below bat access tile-set
15	Reclaimed, locally grown or FSC temperate softwood rafters (avoid trussed rafters), 200 x 50 mm
16	'Schwegler Bat Box 1FE 00748/3', wood-concrete, 300 x 300 x 100 mm
17	'Pro clima Solitex Plus' Roofing underlay
18	Air passage gap, 50 mm
19	FSC timber panel, 600 mm wide
20	Reclaimed, locally sourced clay handmade plain roof tiles 265 x 160 x 10 mm
21	Reclaimed, locally grown or FSC temperate softwood roof tile battens, 25 x 50 m
22	Reclaimed, locally grown or FSC temperate softwood ceiling joist, 200 x 50 mm
23	Gap in underlay below bat access tile set
24	Bat roost fixed to side of rafters below ridge beam, 2 boards spaced apart, 15–20 mm minimum, 25–30 mm maximum
24a	Optional materials: Reclaimed, locally grown or FSC temperate softwood scraps
24b	Optional materials: FSC WBP water boil proof plywood strips
24c	Optional materials: Cement-wood particle board, roughened/grooved surface for climbing and hanging
25	Reclaimed, locally grown or FSC temperate durable species softwood, barge board on softwood spacers, 15–30 mm gap
26	Polythene cavity trap DPC

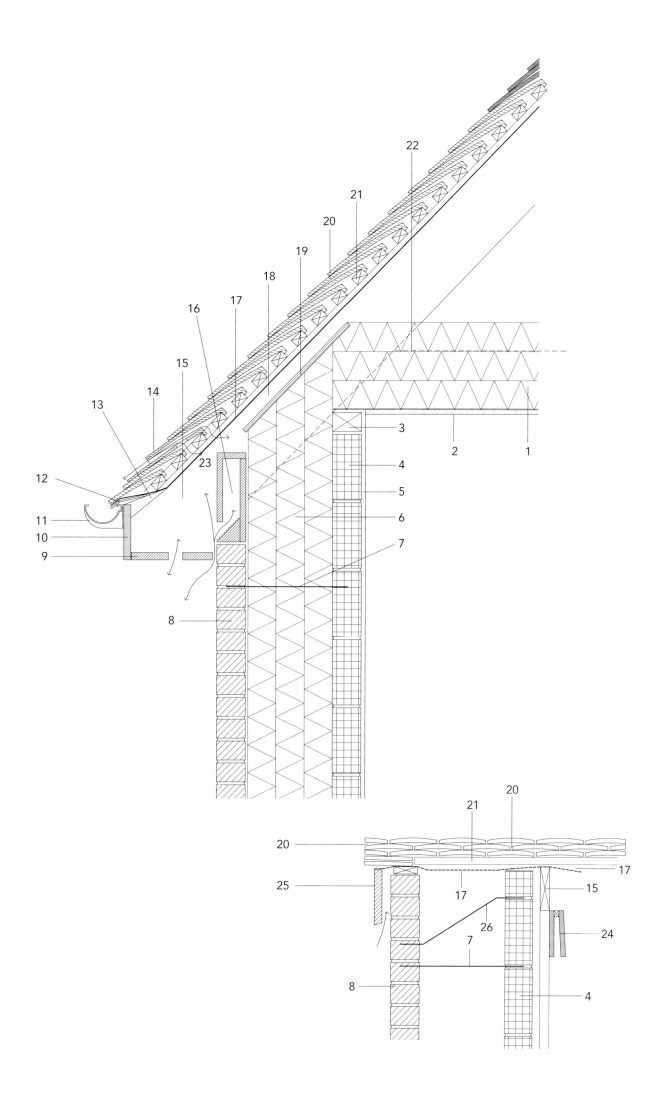

Drawing No. 10
Cavity walls 4 – hemp-lime block and insulated diaphragm wall providing spaces for bats and swifts

1   Hemp insulation, 3 x 100 mm

2   'Pro clima DB+' ATL Air Tightness Layer, recycled paper/cellulose, lapped and natural glued joints

3   Drylining ceiling board

4   Reclaimed, locally grown or FSC temperate softwood wall plate, 75 x 100 mm with holding down straps

5   Cellular blockwork inner leaf, 100 mm

6   Air tight parge coat: clay, lime or gypsum, 5–8 mm or plaster

7   Full fill cavity wall insulation, 3 x 100 mm rock mineral fibre

8   Wall ties option: 2 part long wall tie, austenitic stainless steel (304 equivalent), 400 mm

8a Wall ties option: 'MagmaTech TeploTie Type 4', extruded basalt and fibre long wall tie, 425 x 6.5 dia. mm

9   Reclaimed, locally made fired clay facing brick outer leaf, 102 x 215 x 65 mm

10 Reclaimed, locally grown or FSC temperate durable species softwood soffit

11 Reclaimed, locally grown or FSC temperate durable species softwood fascia

12 Gutter and brackets, galvanized steel, half round

13 Rigid HDPE flashing into gutter

14 Reclaimed, locally grown or FSC temperate softwood tilting fillet, 50 mm x varies

15 'Bat access tile-set', 18 mm gap x 165 mm long, gap in underlay below bat access tile-set

16 Reclaimed, locally grown or FSC temperate softwood rafters (avoid trussed rafters), 200 x 50 mm

17 'Schwegler Bat Box 1FE 00748/3', wood-concrete, 300 x 300 x 100 mm

18 'Pro clima Solitex Plus' Roofing underlay

19 Air passage gap, 50 mm

20 FSC timber panel, 600 mm wide

21 Reclaimed, locally sourced clay handmade plain roof tiles 265 x 160 x 10 mm

22 Reclaimed, locally grown or FSC temperate softwood roof tile battens, 25 x 50 m

23 Reclaimed, locally grown or FSC temperate softwood ceiling joist, 200 x 50 mm

24 Gap in underlay below bat access tile set

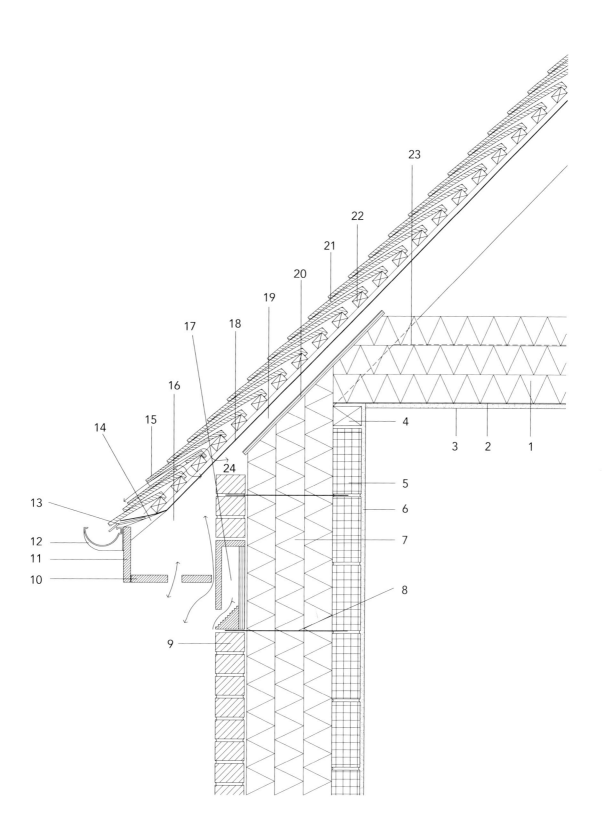

Drawing No. 11
Solid in-situ wall – timber framed and insitu-sprayed hemp-lime infill walls providing spaces for bats and swifts

1   'Schwegler Bat Box 1FE 00748/3', wood-concrete, 300 x 300 x 100 mm. Supported by noggins

2   Reclaimed, locally grown or FSC temperate softwood tiling battens

3   'Pro clima Solitex Plus' WTL Wind Tightness Layer and VPU vapour permeable underlay

4   Reclaimed, locally grown or FSC temperate softwood counter battens, 50 x 25 mm

5   Reclaimed, locally sourced clay plain roof tiling

6   In-situ sprayed hemp-lime mix sprayed against (8) until required thickness of wall achieved, Surface flattened and keyed for (12)

6a   In-situ sprayed hemp-lime mix sprayed against (8) until required thickness of roof achieved, to roof between rafters, Surface smoothed for (2), (3), (4), etc.

7   Reclaimed, locally grown or FSC temperate softwood rafter framing, 140 x 38 @ 600 mm centres

8   Permanent formwork, Moisture tolerant, Moisture permeable

9   Lime or clay plaster (internally) (not cement)

10   Reclaimed, locally grown or FSC temperate softwood stud framing, 140 x 38 @ 600 mm centres at internal face wall

10a   Reclaimed, locally grown or FSC temperate softwood stud framing, 140 x 38 @ 600 mm centres at centre of wall

10b   Reclaimed, locally grown or FSC temperate softwood stud framing, 140 x 38 @ 600 mm centres at external face wall

11   Reclaimed, locally grown or FSC temperate softwood noggins, 50 x 50 mm

12   Lime, hemp-lime or mineral based thin render system 2 layers, reinforcement layer between (airtight and permeable) (not cement)

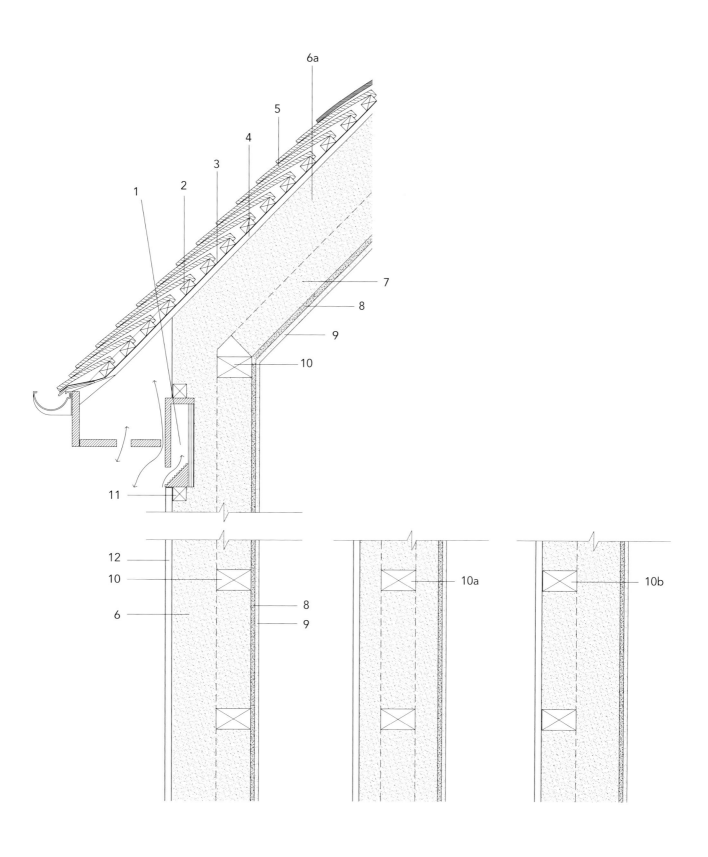

3.12.3 Extruded cellular-fired clay block

Extruded cellular-fired clay block is a build style that originated from mainland Europe. In mainland Europe there is a predominance of nuclear and hydro-electric power stations, so concrete blocks are not a normal part of their industry. In the UK we have a lot of coal-fired power stations which produce a waste product called PFA (pulverised fuel ash) which is used as a cement replacement and a primary aggregate substitute. These have been used to make lower embodied energy ingredients for high embodied energy manufacturing, steam autoclaved, aerated, concrete blocks in the UK. These cellular-fired clay blocks are extruded, creating lots of air cells that trap air and create long path routes through the block for conducted heat, so offering a good U value. The blocks also have thermal mass and moisture mass, helping to moderate both the temperature and humidity of the spaces adjacent to the blocks. Drawing Nos 12 to 14 show the incorporation of the Schwegler product Swift and Bat Box 1MF (see p. 43).

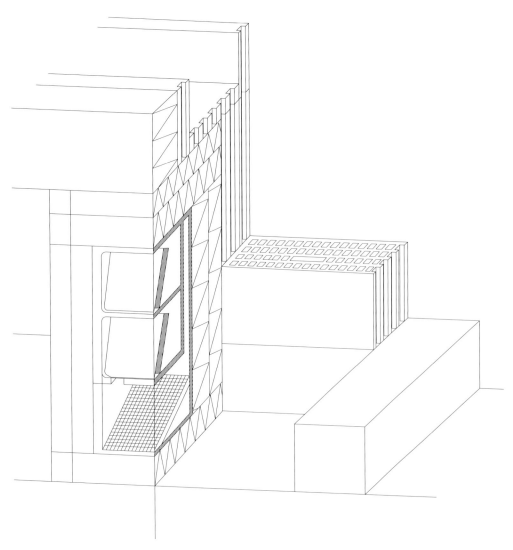

Drawing No. 12
Cellular block 1

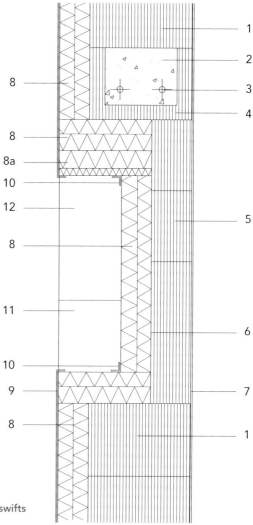

Drawing No. 13

Cellular block 2 – extruded cellular block walling providing spaces for bats and swifts

1 Option: Extruded cellular fired clay block wall, 365 (w) x 250 (h) x 248 (l) mm

1a Option: Extruded cellular lime pumice blocks

2 'Eco-concrete': Less OP cement and more GGBS ground granulated burst furnace slag cement, less virgin aggregate and more recycled, secondary or manufactured aggregate

3 Reinforcement bars

4 Option: Trough lintel: cellular fired clay, 50 mm wall

4a Option: Trough lintel: cellular lime pumice, 50 mm wall

5 Extruded cellular fired clay block leaf, 140 (w) x 300 x 250 (h) mm

6 Cement/clay/adhesive bed joint 1 mm (dry purpends)

7 Airtight parge coat: clay, lime or gypsum, 5–8 mm or plaster

8 Dense wood fibre board, thermal and acoustic insulation board, T&G jointed for air tightness, (no substitution), 100 mm consisting of 4 x 25, 3 x 33 or 2 x 50 mm

8a 75 mm consisting of 3 x 25 mm

9 Lime, hemp-lime or mineral based thin render system 2 layers, reinforcement layer between (airtight and permeable) (not cement)

10 'Pro clima Tescon No. 1 & Tescon Primer RP' Air tight joint taping (option)

11 'Schwegler Bat Ramp', wood-concrete, 250 (h) x 430 (w) x 225 (d) mm

12 'Schwegler Bird/Bat Box', wood-concrete, 460 (h) x 730 (w) x 225 (d) mm. Locate towards eaves. Interlocking and assembled, 700 (h) x 430 (w) x 225 (d) mm (includes (11) above)

Drawing No. 14

Cellular blocks 3 and 4 – extruded cellular fired clay block walling providing spaces for bats and swifts

1   Option: Clay skim/finish, 2 mm

2   'Clayboard' reed reinforced clay drylining board, 40 mm

3   'Dot and dab' bonded drylining

4   Airtight parge coat: clay, lime or gypsum, 5–8 mm or plaster

5   Option: Gypsum plaster skim, 2 mm

6   Option: Plasterboard dry lining, 12.5 mm

6a   Option: Dense gypsum wood fibre reinforced board lining, 10 mm

7   Airtight clay plaster, 20 mm

8   Bed joint: clay/cement/adhesive, 1 mm

8a   Interlocking T&G dry purpend joint, 1 mm (air leaky)

9   Option: Extruded cellular fired clay blocks walling 265 (w) x 250 (h) x 248 (l) mm

9a   Option: Extruded cellular lime pumice blocks

10   Lime, hemp-lime or mineral based thin render system 2 layers, reinforcement layer between (airtight and
        permeable) (not cement)

11   Dense wood fibre board, 25 mm thermal and acoustic insulation, (no substitution permitted)

11a   Same as (11) but a different assembled thickness to (11)

11b   Reclaimed, locally grown or FSC temperate softwood battens and cross battens 50 x 50 and 50 x 75 mm
        (to minimise thermal bridges)

12   'Pro clima Tescon No. 1 and Tescon Primer RP' Air tight joint taping (option)

13   'Schwegler Bat Ramp', wood-concrete, 250 (h) x 430 (w) x 225 (d) mm

14   'Schwegler Swift/Bat Box', wood-concrete, 460 (h) x 430 (w) x 225 (d) mm

13/14   Interlocking assembled: 700 (h) x 430 (w) x 225 (d) mm

15   Option: Trough lintel: cellular fired clay, 50 mm wall

15a   Option: Trough lintel: cellular lime pumice, 50 mm wall

16   Reinforcement bars

17   'Eco-concrete': Less OP cement and more GGBS ground granulated burst furnace slag cement,
        less virgin aggregate and more recycled, secondary or manufactured aggregate

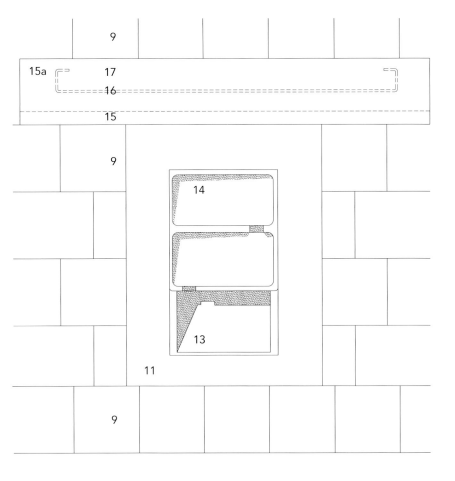

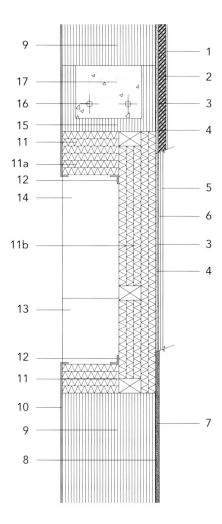

3.12.4 Timber frame

Today the term 'timber frame' is used to describe timber stud framework, usually panellised (sometimes known as cassette panels), which may or may not be pre-insulated. They are usually available as kits or are produced to bespoke designs.

Drawing Nos 15 and 16 show possibilities which allow a crevice-dwelling bat the opportunity to find a range of temperatures. This is not always easy to do in low and zero carbon builds, as the available areas are often only at one depth. The advantage of the design shown in the drawings is that, if conditions become too extreme in the outer-crevice space (extreme heat in mid-summer or very low temperatures during the winter), there is a deeper option that will provide a more stable and moderate temperature range.

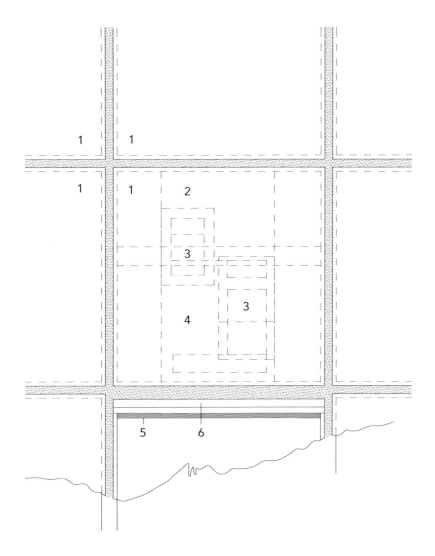

Drawing No. 15
Timber frame 1 with rain screen cladding (elevation)

1   Rainscreen cladding, open joints ventilated cavity, pressure equalised, many material choices, many systems on market

2   Cement-wood particle board, Roughened/grooved surface for climbing and hanging

3   Cement-wood particle board lapped tunnel between roosts, Roughened surface for climbing (but smooth may be okay)

4   'Schwegler Bat Box/entrance 1FE 00747/6', Wood-concrete, 300 x 300 x 80 mm

5   Pressed metal drip or durable FSC hardwood sloping top and drip profile bottom

6   Noggins, durable species softwood to avoid preservative treatment, size to suit

Drawing No. 16
Timber frame 1 – timber stud framed walls (external and internal insulation) providing spaces for bats

1	Dense wood fibre board, thermal and acoustic insulation board, T&G jointed for airtightness; external to stud, 200 mm consisting of 5 No. x 40 mm. Avoids thermal bridges through insulation
1a	Cellulose fibre thermal insulation (easy to cut to shape and to fit odd shaped cavity)
2	Noggins, durable species softwood to avoid preservative treatment, size to suit
3	'Schwegler Bat Box/entrance 1FE 00747/6', wood-concrete, 300 x 300 x 80 mm
3a	'Schwegler Bat Box 1FE 00748/3', wood-concrete, 300 x 300 x 100 mm
4	Cement-wood particle board lapped tunnel between roosts, Roughened surface for climbing (but smooth may be okay)
5	'Pro clima DB+' ATL Air Tightness Layer, Recycled paper/cellulose, lapped and natural glued joints
6	'Clayboard' reed reinforced clay drylining board, 40 mm
7	Clay skim finish, 2 mm
8	Cladding rails/battens, metal, hardwood or durable species softwood to avoid preservative treatment
9	Pressed metal drip or durable FSC hardwood sloping top and drip profile bottom
10	Rainscreen cladding, open joints ventilated cavity, pressure equalised, many material choices, many systems on market
11	Cement-wood particle board, Roughened/grooved surface for climbing and hanging
12	Cavity fire barrier: galvanized mild steel angle; softwood: 50 x 50 mm or plastic sheathed rock mineral fibre
13	Battens, durable species softwood to avoid preservative treatment, 50 x 50 mm @ 600 mm centres
14	'Pro clima Solitex WA' WTL Wind Tightness Layer, lapped and sealed joints
15	Reclaimed, locally grown or FSC temperate softwood stud framing, 140 x 38 mm @ 600 mm centres

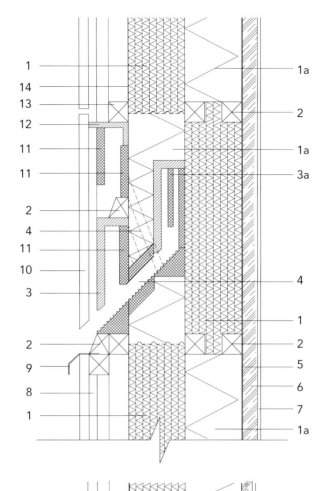

Section

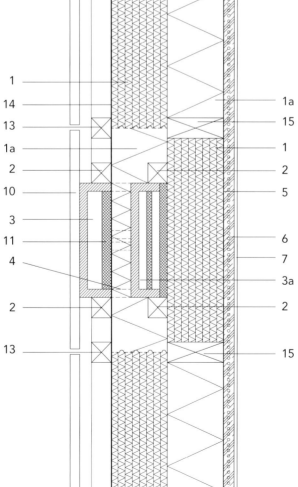

Plan

3.12.5 Insulated structural panel system (ISPs)

The insulated structural panel system (ISPs) is a panelised modern method of construction developed in the UK and championed as part of a system promoted for its enhanced vapour transfer, otherwise known as breathing wall construction. Wet or dry sprayed, or blown in, cellulose fibre insulation is used as a part of the thermal insulation performance. Using a medium performance thermal insulating material means the panel is relatively thick.

Drawing No. 17 details how the ready-made Schwegler product Bat Access panel or roost 1FE (see p. 36) could be incorporated into an ISP build. Of course it does not need to be a ready-made product and, as with all these drawings, it could incorporate a bespoke space.

Drawing No. 17
ISPs 1 and 2 – composite timber I-Stud framed walls providing spaces for bats

1	Reclaimed, locally grown or FSC temperate softwood service zone battens, 30 x 30 mm services and insulation to fill voids
2	'Clayboard' reed reinforced clay drylining board, 40 mm
3	Clay finish, 2 mm
4	'Pro clima DB+' ATL Air Tightness Layer, Recycled paper/cellulose, lapped and natural glued joints
5	'Homatherm flexCL 400', 3 x 100 mm, Dense cellulose fibre, Recycled magazines, Thermal/acoustic insulation
5a	Options: Alternatives: dry or damp spray or blown in insulation, can be pre or post installed
6	Reclaimed, locally grown or FSC temperate durable hardwood, weatherboarding, board on board
7	Pressed metal drip or durable FSC hardwood sloping top and drip profile bottom
8	Cement-wood particle board, 25 mm roughened/grooved for climbing and hanging
9	'Schwegler Bat Box 1FE 00747/6', wood-concrete, 300 x 300 x 80 mm locate towards eaves
10	Breathing Sheathing Board, T&G jointed, with or without racking strength dense wood fibre board, 25 mm
11	'Pro clima Solitex WA' WTL Wind Tightness Layer, lapped and sealed joints
12	Reclaimed, locally grown or FSC temperate durable hardwood battens for weatherboarding, 25 x 50 mm
13	Services in services zone
14	'Masonite I-stud' @ 600 mm, Excel Industries in UK, 300 x 50 mm length to suit, many other sizes available
15	Dense wood fibre board insulation within joint between ISPs, to suit profile or rebate
16	Reclaimed, locally grown or FSC temperate softwood counter-battens, 50 x 50 mm @ 600 centres

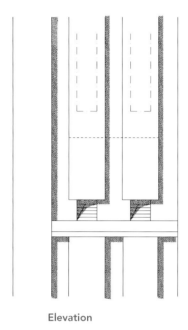

Elevation

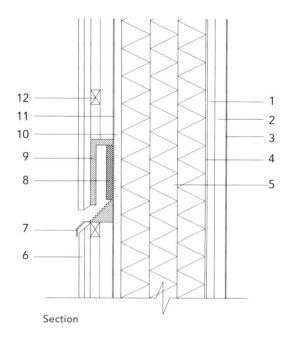

12		1
11		2
10		3
9		4
8		5
7		
6		

Section

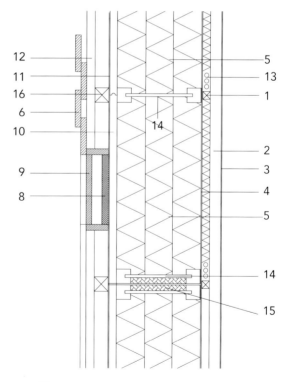

12		5
11		13
16		1
6		
10		
	14	
9		2
8		3
		4
		5
		14
		15

Plan

3.12.6 Structural insulation panel system (SIPs)

The structural insulation panel system (SIPs) is a panelised modern method of construction developed in mainland Europe, and which has been adopted in the UK. Foamed insulation is used as a part of the structural performance of the panel, thus enabling a reduced thickness of the panel. The insulation is foamed into the panel, but there are alternative methods of making them using laminated construction.

For structural insulation panel systems there is limited space to work with, but even here it is possible to include ready-made (as illustrated by the Schwegler product Bat Access Panel or roost 1FE (see p. 36)) or bespoke roost spaces.

Drawing No. 18
Structural Insulation Panel system (SIPs) providing spaces for bats

1	Drylining gypsum plasterboard, 12.5 mm and 2 mm skim or flush taped and filled joints
2	Structural Insulated Panel
2a	Non-renewable, foamed plastics insulation
2b	Or laminated assembly with adhesive
2c	FSC OSB or other timber panel, both sides
3	Pressed metal drip
4	'Schwegler Bat Box 1FE 00747/6', wood-concrete, 300 x 300 x 80 mm locate towards eaves
5	Cement-wood particle board, 12 mm roughened surface for climbing/hanging
6	Reclaimed, locally grown or FSC temperate softwood noggins, 50 x 50 mm
7	Insect resistant mesh/perforated metal
8	Cladding (numerous systems on market)
9	Cladding rails/battens. Could be timber weather boarding (shown) (numerous systems on market)
10	'Pro clima Rapidcell' Air tight jointing tape to joints
11	Reclaimed, locally grown or FSC temperate softwood pressure batten, (internal), 50 x 50 mm to secure airtight seal (10 above)
12	Note, do not try to make airtight with sealant gun afterwards, little hope, unless bottomless funds and open-ended programme
13	Reclaimed, locally grown or FSC temperate softwood durable species, pressure batten, 50 x 50 mm to secure wind-tight seal (14 below)
14	'Pro clima Tescon No.1' Wind tightness tape to joints
15	Interlocking joint, Tight fit ideally, Airtight ideally (probably not), See (13) + (14) & (10) + (11)

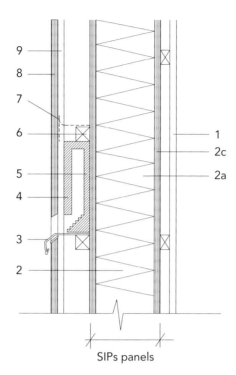

9
8
7
6
5
4
3
2

1
2c
2a

Section

SIPs panels

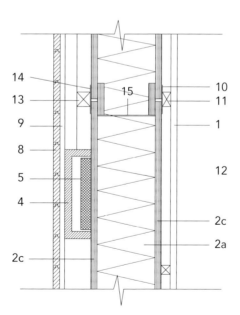

14
13
9
8
5
4

2c

15

10
11

1

12

2c
2a

Plan

3.12.7 Insulating concrete formwork (ICF)

Insulating concrete formwork (ICF) is a small-scale modular formwork system that uses thermal insulation in place of plywood, and which also has a system to hold the two forms together and apart at the required distance, using a variety of different methods as diverse as reinforcement cages or plastic ties. The space in between is filled with reinforcing rods and in-situ concrete to make insulated structural load-bearing walls. Some systems are restricted to straight walls and right angles, others have curves. This method of wall construction is often adopted by self-builders because it is lightweight, easy to handle, simple and fast.

Although designs for crevice-dwelling bats were developed, it was not felt that there was sufficient confidence in finding ways in which to: (a) maintain the necessary level of thermal insulation in a standard way; and (b) to acoustically isolate the bats from the interior of the building. So, for these reasons, it has been decided not to include the drawings in this book at this time. It is recognised that construction using ICF will have a place in future low and zero carbon buildings, and therefore further development of the appropriate biodiversity provision that meets all necessary considerations will be continued as a collaborative work in progress.

3.12.8 Cross-laminated timber panels (CLTP)

Cross-laminated timber panels (CLTP) is a method of construction originating from mainland Europe that makes use of forest thinnings of small section. It usually consists of same-sized square battens bonded to create a sheet one batten thick. To this is added two or more layers of the same, but each layer is arranged at right angles to the previous layer, and all are adhered to each other. This makes a very strong, dimensionally stable, rigid panel from which structural panels are cut to size and shape. They are used for floors, walls, roofs and partitions, and even for stairs. Holes for doors and windows are cut out. The panels are assembled in relation to each other and are secured to each other with galvanized steel angles and nuts and bolts. It is a rapid method of construction with limitations, but it is possible to incorporate a space for our building reliant wildlife.

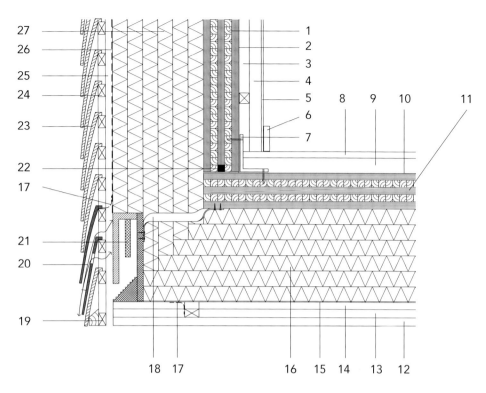

Drawing No. 19

Cross-Laminated Timber Panel (CLTP) system –
one- or two-storey carport/passageway providing spaces for bats

1   CLTP Cross-Laminated Timber Panel wall, 125 mm. FSC plywood core, 25 mm. FSC temperate plantation thinings softwood battens 25 x 25 mm. One or more layers each side of ply

2   'Pro clima Intello Plus' ATL lapped bonded

3   Reclaimed, locally grown or FSC temperate softwood service batten, 30 x 30 mm services and insulation

4   Option: 'Clayboard' reed reinforced clay drylining board, 40 mm

4a   Option: Plasterboard dry lining, 12.5 mm

5   Clay skim/finish, 2 mm

6   Reclaimed, locally grown or FSC temperate softwood or FSC ZF MDF Zero Formaldehyde Medium Density Fibreboard skirting, 20 x 100 mm

7   GMS galvanized mild steel angle cleats and screws

8   Reclaimed, locally grown or FSC temporary durable hardwood or softwood T&G board

9   Dense wood fibre board, thermal/acoustic insulation boards, 50 mm. T&G jointed

10   'Pro clima Intello Plus' ATL Air Tightness Layer lapped bonded

11   CLTP Cross-Laminated Timber Panel floor, 125 mm. FSC plywood core, 25 mm. FSC temperate plantation thinings softwood battens 25 x 25 mm. One or more layers each side of ply

12   Reclaimed, locally grown or FSC temporary durable hardwood weather boarding, 25 mm. No finish

13   Reclaimed, locally grown or FSC temperate softwood battens, 50 x 25 mm for weather boarding

14   Reclaimed, locally grown or FSC temperate softwood counter battens, 50 x 25 mm

15   'Pro clima Solitex Plus' WTL Wind Tightness Layer and VPU vapour permeable underlay

16   Dense wood fibre board, thermal and acoustic insulation, 6 x 50 mm

17   Insect resistant mesh to isolate air spaces (locate higher to offer more space for bats on wall)

18   GMS galvanized mild steel fixing strap screwed to background and box

19   Reclaimed, locally grown or FSC temperate softwood tilting fillet for bottom of tiling to maintain tile slope angle and bat access

20   'Bat access tile-set', 18 mm gap x 165 mm long, gap in underlay below bat access tile-set

21   'Schwegler Bat Box 1FE 00748/3', wood-concrete, 300 x 300 x 100 mm

22   'Compriband' Pre-compressed impregnated foam, self-adhesive in 25 mm x 25 mm channel in (1)

23   Tile hanging or weather boarding (see also 20 above)

24   Reclaimed, locally grown or FSC temperate softwood battens, 50 x 25 mm

25   Reclaimed, locally grown or FSC temperate softwood counter battens, 50 x 50 mm

26   'Pro clima Solitex Plus' WTL Wind Tightness Layer and VPU vapour permeable underlay

27   Dense wood fibre board, thermal and acoustic insulation, 6 x 50 mm

Living roof

3.13 Living roofs and walls

Living roofs and walls are common in Switzerland and Germany, and there is a growing number now found in London and in other major cities in the UK.

3.13.1 Roofs

Benefits of living roofs

The area of roofs in an urban environment are considerable and tend to be sterile environments, largely uninviting for biodiversity and not pleasant to look at from upstairs windows. Living roofs can support a whole range of invertebrates, depending on the type of roof grown. There will be generalist insects, such as ladybird species, bees and grasshoppers, but there is also a possibility of supporting more uncommon species, including moth and butterfly species not normally found in the conditions present in gardens. The array of insects and the seeds produced by the flowering plants all provide good feeding opportunities to a range of birds, from common garden birds, such as greenfinch, blackbirds and wrens, to goldfinch, linnets and even the rare black redstarts in certain parts of the country. This proliferation of insects is also likely to be a feature that will be of benefit to foraging bats, as all the UK bats are insectivorous. A bird particularly associated with living roofs is the black redstart. This has a limited distribution in the UK, predominantly being found in London, Birmingham and the Black Country. In these urban areas it can be very beneficial for the populations of black redstart if living roofs, which meet the needs of this species, are incorporated. Details of these needs can be found on the specialist website www.blackredstarts.org.uk.

In addition to these benefits for biodiversity, living roofs have other positive benefits such as moderating the temperature of the rooms beneath, helping to keep them cool in warm weather and insulating them against cold. In heavy or prolonged rainfall, living roofs reduce the likelihood of floods by acting as a sponge that absorbs water before allowing it to evaporate back into the atmosphere. Living roofs also protect the roof material from the effects of ultra-violet light and frost that could be damaging.

Types of living roof

Mosses and lichens naturally colonise roofs and establish themselves in the harshest of environments without substrate or support. Roofs that have moss and lichen will host a whole range of associated invertebrates and microscopic creatures, which are, in turn, a valuable food source for birds. It is possible to obtain pre-grown moss mats, but more often it is a case of not being over tidy with what will naturally colonise a roof. Besides these naturally occurring colonists, it is possible to create a living roof on a new or existing building (structure permitting).

Black Redstart

There are a range of living roofs available, but they fall under the broad categories of: shallow, which imitates the harsh environments such as cliffs and mountains; and deep roofs, which, due to the deeper growing substrate, allow a greater range of plants to be grown that, in turn, can support a greater range of biodiversity, but they do require more maintenance. Very deep roofs have a depth of substrate sufficient to allow shrubs and even trees to grow, and are less often likely to be a viable option.

A living roof comprises a number of layers, generally a waterproof layer, a root barrier, a filter layer, moisture blanket, drainage layer, the soil mixture and the planting layer.

Where can they be used?

A flat roof is ideal, although other types of roof may be possible to utilise as long as the slope is not too severe.

3.13.2 Walls

Benefits of living walls

Whereas roofs are often not a visible feature from the ground level, we are more aware of walls in our towns and cities. Living walls utilise plants in order to derive benefits, not only in visual terms, but also in regard to biodiversity, thermal efficiency and the reduction of pollutants. By providing shading from the sun, living walls can significantly reduce the external temperature of a building. Living walls can also provide a certain amount of insulation, although the effectiveness of this will depend on the type and structure of the living wall and the overall energy performance of the building itself. Living walls can also help reduce the urban heat island effect by intercepting heat which would otherwise be largely absorbed and radiated by the building surfaces back into the surroundings. They also help to shield the surface from ultra-violet light, which could be an important consideration for some modern cladding materials.

Living wall

Plants on buildings can potentially provide a food source for invertebrates on which, in turn, other invertebrates, bats and birds may feed. They also provide a breeding and nesting habitat for invertebrates and birds, and are ideal for including ready-made nest boxes.

Types of living wall

As with living roofs, there is nothing new in the concept of using plants to green buildings, but in recent years a variety of modern designs and techniques have been developed. Living walls can be separated into a number of categories that include:

- supported by a wall – self-supporting climbers;
- supported by a structure on a wall – trellis, etc.;
- supported by a self-standing structure away from a wall – frameworks, etc.;
- hanging walls – allowing plants to hang from a height; and
- walls with plants growing within them.

Considerations in the use of living walls

The use of planted climbers, either self-supporting or in some way trained against a wall or similar structure, is not a new idea and, as long as the choice of plant is wise for the position and soil type, then it is a tried and tested way of greening a wall. The techniques used where the planted material is supported within the wall structure is not so well understood and some of the earlier designs of planted walls have declined over time, with the occasional outright failure. This is not to say that green walls are high risk, but it is prudent to ensure that an experienced practitioner is consulted and that an understanding of any need for ongoing maintenance is acknowledged if the plants are not rooted in the ground.

A great deal more information can be found on the following websites:

- www.livingroofs.org;
- www.london.gov.uk (search for 'living roofs' and 'walls pdf'); and
- http://naturalengland.etraderstores.com (search for living roofs).

3.14 How many is enough?

There is never going to be a 'one-size-fits-all' answer to this question. It is a case of taking the advice of an experienced ecologist who has carried out a survey of the site in question and its surroundings, and who can advise on the species for which it is appropriate to make provision and on how, where and how many potential roosts/nesting sites should be incorporated. However, having said that, the recent Eco-towns biodiversity worksheet, published by the Town and Country Planning Association (TCPA) in December 2009, has included a table that gives some guidance as to the likely level of provision expected. This table is replicated in Table 3.16.

Table 3.16: Recommended roost and nest provision for building reliant species in Eco-towns (TCPA, 2009)

Potentially appropriate species (depending on location)	Recommended number of roosts/nest sites
Crevice-dwelling bats	1 in 20 structures
Bats requiring flight space	1 in 5 public buildings (non-residential)
Horseshoe bats	1 in 5 public buildings (non-residential)
Swifts	1 in 20 buildings
House martins	1 in 50 buildings
House sparrows	1 in 40 buildings
Starlings	1 in 100 buildings
Swallows	1 in 50 buildings
Barn owls	2 per medium-size development 3 per large development
Peregrine falcons	1 per medium-size development 2 per large development

chapter four

Additional information

This book is all about helping to ensure that our future buildings are not devoid of the biodiversity that has so long been associated with them, and which are an important component of a sustainable built environment. Having explored solutions to the threats to biodiversity that have incidentally arisen as a result of the need to reduce the carbon footprint of our buildings, for completeness other aspects of new developments that make a real difference to biodiversity are now briefly included. Some of these are areas where knowledge and advice already exists, and where this is the case the source of that information is highlighted.

4.1 Artificial lighting

4.1.1 The bigger picture

Wherever human habitation spreads, so does artificial lighting. However, this increase in lighting has been shown to have an adverse effect on our British wildlife, particularly on those species that have evolved to be active during the hours of darkness. So any development needs to carefully consider what lighting is necessary and reduce any unnecessary lighting, both temporally and spatially. The good news is that, when the impacts on a range of species groups are reviewed, the solutions proposed have commonalities that form the basis of good practice. Firstly, to review some of the impacts on British species groups.

4.1.2 Moths

The findings of a report on the population trends of 337 species of moth between 1968 and 2002 are a matter for concern, with 67% of common and widespread moth species having declined and 21% considered endangered or vulnerable. Habitat changes in extent and quality are the prime suspects for the decline, along with pesticide use, eutrophication (the depletion of oxygen in water due to excessive nutrients in water, usually from fertilisers or sewage) affecting plant composition, climate change and light pollution. When looking at population levels, it is not always easy to disentangle the effects of lighting on moths from other impacts of urbanisation, but there are known effects that lighting has on moth behaviour. Many moth species are sensitive to light at the ultra-violet (UV) end of the spectrum. Where a light source has this UV component, male moths in particular will be drawn to it.

Red Underwing moth

Most light-induced changes in physiology and behaviour are likely to be detrimental. However, even without this UV element, so attractive to moths, the mere presence of even near monochromatic light will affect the behaviour of certain moth species. They still discern it to be 'light', so they are completely inhibited and do not fly to feed or mate.

Advice from Rothamsted Research (Kelvin Conrad, personal communication) suggests the following mitigating steps:

- Keep the wattage low and reduce UV, perhaps using low UV LED lights.
- Only use light where and when needed – minimise glare and overspill lighting, limit lighting to the intended surfaces and avoid spill light onto ponds, hedges and trees.
- Use tightly sealed units so that insects cannot become trapped within the unit.

4.1.3 Birds

When considering the impacts of lighting on birds, there are several aspects of changes to bird behaviour to take into account. The phenomenon of robins and other birds singing by the light of a street light is well known, and research by Alex Pollard of the University of Cardiff (Pollard, 2009) found that singing did not have a significant effect on the bird's body mass regulation. However, it was felt that the continual lack of sleep was likely to be detrimental to the birds' survival and could disrupt the long-term circadian rhythm that dictates the onset of the breeding season. It also has the potential to cause hormone disruption. The advice for mitigation is to minimise light spill and use lights only where and when needed.

Other UK bird species known to be sensitive to artificial lighting are long-eared owls, black-tailed godwit and stone curlew. In a study in Spain over an eight-year period (Rodríguez et al., 2006), it was found that long-eared owls selected nest sites that were not in lit areas.

Some birds have changed their behaviour to adapt to artificial lighting. In the case of peregrine falcons, Edward Drewitt, a researcher based in Bristol, has found that the peregrines which have moved into cities and use tall buildings as a substitute for cliffs have made a further adjustment in their behaviour. In examining the prey remains taken from a number of feeding sites, Drewitt and Dixon (2008) found clear evidence of prey species caught at night.

Another opportunist bird, the gull, has also found street lighting can be to its advantage. In our towns and cities, gulls are known to leave at dusk to roost elsewhere, only to return hours later to feed on the discarded takeaways before the refuse collectors have a chance to clear them.

Many species of bird migrate at night and there are well-documented cases of the mass mortality of these nocturnal migrating birds at tall lit structures on an international scale.

Robin

4.1.4 Mammals

Most of our British mammals are nocturnal and have adapted their lifestyle so that they are active in the dark in order to avoid predators. Artificial illumination of the areas in which these mammals are active and foraging is likely to be disturbing to their normal activities and their foraging areas could be lost in this way. It is thought that the most pronounced effect is likely to be on small mammals due to their need to avoid predators. However, this in itself has a knock-on effect on those predators.

The group of mammals upon which the detrimental effect of artificial lighting is most clearly seen is bats. Our 17 British bat species native to the UK have all suffered dramatic reductions in their numbers in the past century. The effect of light falling on a bat roost access point, regardless of which species of UK bats resides there, will be to at least delay bats from emerging, which shortens the amount of time available to them for foraging. As the main peak of nocturnal insect abundance occurs at and soon after dusk, a delay in emergence means this vital time for feeding is missed. At worst, the bats may feel compelled to abandon the roost. Bats are faithful to their roosts over many years and disturbance of this sort can have a significant effect on the future of the colony. It is likely to be deemed a breach of the national and European legislation that protects British bats and their roosts.

Flying bat

In addition to causing disturbance to bats at the roost, artificial lighting can also affect the feeding behaviour of bats and their use of commuting routes. There are two aspects to this: one is the attraction that UV light has to a range of insects; the other is the presence of lit conditions.

As previously indicated, many night-flying species of insect are attracted to lamps that emit an UV component. Studies have shown that, although noctules, Leisler's, serotines and pipistrelle bats take advantage of the concentration of insects around white street lights as a source of prey, this behaviour is not true for all bat species. The slower flying, broad-winged species, such as long-eared bats, barbastelle bats, greater and lesser horseshoe bats and the *Myotis* species (which include Brandt's, whiskered, Daubenton's, Natterer's and Bechstein's) generally avoid street lights. To compound the situation, it is also thought that insects are attracted to lit areas from further afield. This could result in adjacent habitats supporting reduced numbers of insects, thereby causing a further impact on the ability of light-avoiding bats to feed. It is noticeable that most of Britain's rarest bats are among those species listed as avoiding light.

Lighting can be particularly harmful if it illuminates important foraging habitats such as river corridors, woodland edges and hedgerows used by bats. Studies have shown that continuous lighting along roads creates barriers which some bat species will not cross. Stone *et al.* (2009) used an experimental approach to provide the first evidence of a negative effect of artificial light pollution on the commuting behaviour of a threatened bat species. High-pressure sodium lights were installed that mimic the intensity and light spectra of streetlights along commuting routes of lesser horseshoe bats (*Rhinolophus hipposideros*). Bat activity was reduced dramatically and the onset of commuting behaviour was delayed in the presence of lighting, with no evidence of habituation. These results demonstrate that light pollution may have significant negative impacts upon the selection of flight routes by bats.

These are just a few examples of the effects of artificial lighting on British wildlife, with migratory fish, amphibians, some flowering plants, a number of bird species, glow worms and a range of other invertebrates all exhibiting changes in their behaviour as a result of this unnatural lighting. When reviewing the currently held view of good practice across a range of UK species, the following do appear to be points of consensus:

- Reduce or remove the UV component of light emitted. To achieve this use either a lamp that does not emit UV or by use of filtration products.
- Avoid light spill (especially onto sensitive habitats), thereby creating not just a green infrastructure, but a dark green infrastructure. This can be achieved by the design of the luminaire and by using accessories such as hoods, cowls, louvres and shields to direct the light to the intended area only. Planting or man-made barriers can also act as protection against light spill. Computer programs used with wildlife in mind can predict where the light cone and spill will occur.
- Use timers to reduce the hours lit, and tailor this specifically to wildlife that would be affected.
- In addition, with advances in technology, such as LED lighting being more widely used, it is now possible in certain circumstances to have lighting that responds to need by detecting the presence of pedestrians.

Of course, the detrimental effect on our wildlife is not the only reason for reviewing the provision of lighting in the built environment. The Campaign for Dark Skies (CfDS) was set up by concerned members of the British Astronomical Association in 1989 to counter the ever-growing tide of skyglow which has tainted the night sky over Britain since the 1950s. Usually the result of poorly aimed streetlights and floodlights emitting light above the horizontal into the sky, skyglow is nowadays increasingly a result of over-powered, poorly mounted household security lights and literally 'over-the-

Illuminated hedge

top' sports lighting. In addition, street lighting is a large energy user and, in an effort to reduce our carbon footprint, it is important to eliminate any unnecessary or wasteful lighting. It is the shared aim of the CfDS, those concerned about our carbon footprint, conservationists and the Institution of Lighting Engineers to see the right amount of light, where needed and when needed.

For more information on lighting and wildlife see:

- the Institution of Lighting Engineers (ILE) – www.ile.org.uk;
- the Bat Conservation Trust (BCT) – www.bats.org.uk;
- the Campaign for Dark Skies (CfDS) – www.britastro.org/dark-skies; and
- the Bats and Lighting Research project – www.batsandlighting.co.uk/index.html.

4.2 Planting for wildlife

'Private gardens collectively cover about 667,000 acres (270,000 hectares) in Britain and make up the largest urban greenspace; ten per cent of the land cover of the UK is urban and it is home to 80 per cent of the population.' (Wembridge, 2007)

The UK's 15 million gardens already provide important homes for wildlife, but the potential for use by wildlife could be much improved. Many creatures that are declining in the countryside, such as the common frog, song thrush and hedgehog, can thrive in domestic gardens and other urban areas if the right conditions are provided. It is possible, with a little more consideration, to make parts of gardens into areas that play a vital role in supporting biodiversity in the urban environment, either as a permanent home, seasonal abode, a place to feed, breed or as part of green infrastructure. There are good publications and websites that provide information on this subject, but there are some key principles that can be followed and these have been grouped into: those that apply during the design stage of the development; and those that can be applied post-occupancy by subsequent occupants.

4.2.1 What can be incorporated during the outline design stage

As part of the outline design, it is important to incorporate green spaces and parks where possible. Natural England has developed the Urban Greenspace Standards (Handley *et al.*, 2003), which recommend that people living in towns and cities should have:

- an accessible natural greenspace less than 300 m (five-minute walk) from home;
- a local nature reserve at a minimum level of 1 ha per thousand population; and
- at least one accessible 20 ha site within 2 km of home, one accessible 100 ha site within 5 km of home, and one accessible 500 ha site within 10 km of home.

Green infrastructure refers to a network of high-quality green spaces and environmental features, including parks, open spaces, playing fields, woodlands, allotments and private gardens. These provide a combination of social, economic and environmental benefits for local communities.

Allotments

Therefore, green infrastructure should be an integral part of all new development. Where these components of green infrastructure are linked, it will give additional benefits to wildlife.

More information can be found in Natural England's guidance on how to design, incorporate and operate green infrastructure, see *NE176 – Natural England's Green Infrastructure Guidance*, which can be found on the Natural England website (www.naturalengland.org.uk). Also see guidance on green infrastructure by searching for 'eco-towns green infrastructure worksheet' at www.tcpa.org.uk.

Other important biodiversity considerations are as follows:

- Having water features of any kind within a development which will be beneficial for wildlife.
- When considering planting, use native trees, shrubs and flowers, as these have more chance of supporting biodiversity. Shrubs with nectar, pollen or fruits are especially attractive to insects or provide food for birds and other animals.
- There is a growing trend for allotment gardening as more people want to grow their own produce and enjoy the additional benefits of healthy outdoor activity. A further benefit is for our wildlife. Allotments can become oases that add to the network of gardens and parks in the urban environment. In particular, where allotment gardening is carried out organically, then the importance for wildlife becomes far greater. So a development that includes the provision of community allotments will have multiple benefits.

What can be encouraged beyond the construction phase

This looks at ways of ensuring that the biodiversity element of sustainable building is continued beyond the direct involvement of the design and development team. Advice on increasing biodiversity in gardens and green spaces is offered from various conservation organisations. The RSPB offers a range of advice for planning and creating a wildlife-friendly garden, including creating a range of habitats, planting shrubs and trees to attract wildlife, and putting up bird boxes. Also, search for 'wildlife gardening' on the following websites, all of which have a host of information:

- www.rspb.org.uk
- www.wildaboutgardens.org.uk
- www.wildlifetrusts.org
- www.bats.org.uk
- www.buglife.org.uk
- www.naturalengland.org.uk (search for plants for wildlife friendly gardens or wildlife on allotments).

4.3 Community involvement

In any new development it is desirable to help the cohesion and inclusive community spirit for the occupants. Projects that involve biodiversity enhancement are an excellent way of doing this and they have additional health and well-being benefits. Environmental projects with community involvement have become increasingly popular, and, over the past few years, a range of grants and funding programmes have been made available for these projects. Approximately 80% of people live in urban areas, and for most of these people local green spaces provide the best opportunities for contact with nature. Projects can include gardening schemes, allotment projects and park planting, among others. These projects establish connections with nature and they use the natural environment to engage with and benefit people and communities. Environmental projects, in particular, have been proven to successfully involve the public, encourage volunteering, raise awareness, and educate and engage new people – all bringing substantial benefits to individuals and the wider community alike. One such project is the Count Bat Project in England, run through the Bat Conservation Trust (BCT). Their aim is to engage, educate and involve as wide a spectrum of people as possible in bat conservation. This involves developing links between the existing bat community, voluntary organisations and local communities. Events have taken place across England and have included bat walks, building bat boxes, bat-friendly planting and bat fun days. Communities actively engaged in bat conservation have opened up to the wider natural environment and its associated benefits.

More information on setting up a community involvement project is available by searching the following websites:

- www.wildlifetrusts.org; and
- www.cabe.org.uk (see their publications *It's Our Space* (2007), *Making Contracts Work for Wildlife* (2006) and *Start with the Park* (2005b)).

4.3.1 Gardens

There are a number of garden projects which encourage community involvement. The British Trust for Ornithology (BTO) run a Garden Bird Watch Programme which requires only basic knowledge and involves collecting simple records of birds seen in a garden. They also run a Nest Record Scheme, which uses simple techniques and so is accessible to everyone, helping to encourage and involve newcomers in a community group. Similarly, together with the BTO, BBC Breathing Places run a project called the Nest Box Challenge. Community groups (or individuals) can register nest boxes in their local area and record what is inside at regular intervals. The RSPB also runs a number of garden-related projects, including Homes for Wildlife. This involves individuals or groups making their gardens and local green spaces richer in wildlife by activities such as putting up nesting boxes, digging ponds and planting trees.

A recent initiative from Natural England is 'The Big Wildlife Garden' (see www.bwg.naturalengland.org.uk). The site recognises the fact that gardens represent an important area of natural habitat for many species, and that gardening in a wildlife-friendly manner can considerably increase the diversity of plants and animals in every garden. The Big Wildlife Garden is free for anyone of any age to join and is open to individuals, schools or community groups.

4.3.2 School involvement

BBC Breathing Places have launched a programme for schools, which is designed to inspire and educate children about wildlife and encourages them to make their school a 'wildlife haven' (see www.bbc.co.uk/breathingplaces/schools). There are a range of suggestions for activities, including planting seeds and trees, building compost bins, and putting up bird and bat boxes. In addition, Natural England's 'The Big Wildlife Garden' has a category for school involvement.

4.3.3 Watching and counting wildlife

BBC Breathing Places also run a community programme. Villages, towns, cities and counties across the UK will soon be able to sign up to make space for nature (www.bbc.co.uk/breathingplaces/communities). Activities will be closely linked between local councils and communities, and will include planting trees, holding events, and building wildlife homes.

NBMP survey

The Bat Conservation Trust run the National Bat Monitoring Programme and the Count Bat project, and both provide opportunities for individuals and communities alike to observe and count wildlife in the field (www.bats.org.uk). Bat sightings can be recorded at www.bats.org.uk/bigbatmap.

4.4 Monitoring and research

Understanding the effects of a development on the biodiversity found within and adjacent to its footprint is important for reporting on biodiversity change as a result of planning consents (see Section 2.2) and this may be carried out by the project ecologist. However, any information recorded in a methodical way with regard to changes in the abundance and diversity of species and habitats will prove valuable in learning about the impact of aspects of development and how best to maximise a positive outcome. A selection of recording techniques available to all is included below, and a number of these could serve the dual purpose of encouraging community involvement and cohesion.

4.4.1 The National Bat Monitoring Programme

The National Bat Monitoring Programme, organised by the Bat Conservation Trust since 1996, runs a number of national, annual surveys through a volunteer network of over 2,000 dedicated volunteers. The core surveys are: the colony count survey (volunteers count bats emerging from roosts at sunset); the hibernation survey (licensed bat workers identify and count bats found in hibernation sites, such as tunnels and caves in winter); and the field and waterway surveys (volunteers count bat passes while walking transects). These are aimed at all skill levels from beginner to expert, and repeat visits are carried out at each site in order to produce statistically robust long-term trends (www.bats.org.uk).

School involvement

4.4.2 Garden bird surveys

Both the Royal Society for the Protection of Birds (RSPB) and the British Trust for Ornithology (BTO) run monitoring programmes. These require a variety of skill levels, but some of these, such as the BTO Garden Bird Watch Programme and Nest Record Scheme, require only basic knowledge and time enough during each week to observe birds in the householder's own garden. Other surveys include the Breeding Bird Survey (which is the main source of population trend information about the UK's widespread birds), BirdTrack and the Nest Box challenge (www.bto.org and www.rspb.org.uk).

4.4.3 Butterfly transects and counting moths

Butterfly Conservation runs ongoing programmes to monitor butterflies in the UK, which involves over 10,000 volunteer recorders. The data gathered are used by the Government to indicate the health of the environment. The surveys are aimed at both beginners and experienced recorders. Data are collected annually to monitor changes in the abundance of butterflies, using the well–established transect methodology – volunteers walk a transect and record butterflies along the route on a regular basis for a number of years. Other surveys simply require volunteers to submit records of sightings from their back garden, and there are also counts for moths to improve knowledge and conservation of the larger moths in the UK. This is a simple survey to record moth sightings and submit these to Butterfly Conservation (www.butterfly-conservation.org).

Jargon buster

The author wishes to acknowledge substantial input from GreenSpec in preparing this jargon buster and also the use of material from the Scottish Environmental Design Association (SEDA), the Ecos Renews and Environmental Building Solutions.

Air barrier
Comprises materials and/or components which are air impervious or virtually so, separating conditioned spaces (heated, cooled or humidity controlled, usually inside) from unconditioned spaces (unheated, un-cooled, humidity uncontrolled, usually outside).

Air exfiltration
The uncontrolled outward leakage of indoor air through cracks, discontinuities and other unintentional openings in the building envelope. In winter the air is likely to be heated, and heated air exfiltration will result in uncontrolled heat loss and potential interstitial condensation risk.

Air infiltration
The uncontrolled inward leakage of outdoor air through cracks, discontinuities and other unintentional openings in the building envelope. In winter the air is likely to be cold, and cold air infiltration will result in uncontrolled draughts, leading to thermal discomfort and condensation risk.

Air leakage path
A route by which air enters or leaves a building, or flows through a component, and can destroy the integrity of the fabric's acoustic, fire, thermal, wind, weather, water and air-tightness performance. During the heating season, air passing through air leakage paths will carry heat, increase energy demand and increase the carbon footprint of the building and its occupants.

Air-tightness
This relates to the 'leakiness' of a building. The smaller the leakage for a given pressure difference across a building, the tighter the building envelope.

Air-tightness layer
A layer built into the external envelope to minimise air infiltration/exfiltration. It may consist of a wide range of materials (e.g. sealants, gaskets, glazing or membranes) and should be continuous to be effective.

Ancient semi-natural woodland
These are woodlands that have persisted in the landscape since the Middle Ages, from a date of approximately 1600AD.

BAP – Biodiversity Action Plan
Describes the UK's biological resources, and commits a detailed plan for conserving and enhancing species and habitats, in addition to promoting public awareness and contributing to international conservation efforts. Species and Habitat Action Plans (SAPs and HAPs) have been drawn up for the UK's most threatened (i.e. priority) species and habitats. See the UK BAP website (www.ukbap.org.uk) and BCT website (www.bats.org.uk) for further information.

BARS – Biodiversity Action Reporting System
This is the UK's Biodiversity Action Plan reporting system. It includes national, local and company Biodiversity Action Plans (BAPs) and all UK Biodiversity Strategies and Action Plans. Reports on status and trends, as well as targets and outcomes for species on the UK BAP list are available to download on the Biodiversity Action Reporting System (www.ukbap-reporting.org.uk/default.asp).

Bat boxes
Artificial roosts, usually made of wood or woodcrete (a mixture of wood chips and concrete). They are designed to provide bats with alternative resting places to replace natural ones in tree holes, and also to encourage bats into areas where there are few such natural sites.

Biodiversity
Biodiversity (biological diversity) is the number and variety of all living organisms, including genetic, species and ecosystem diversity. It includes all wildlife, plants, bacteria and viruses, and their habitats, and this variety is vital to a well-functioning ecosystem.

BREEAM
BREEAM (BRE Environmental Assessment Method) is a Sustainability Assessment Tool. Sustainability assessment tools are used to measure sustainability of a construction or building, including the contribution played by recycled and secondary aggregates, via an index or scoring system.

Carbon sequestration
Carbon sequestration in construction usually refers to building products derived from plant materials such as wood and hemp, where CO_2 is absorbed as part of the growing process. The carbon remains 'locked' in the material for the lifetime of the building; if designed for deconstruction and reused, the carbon remains 'locked' for longer.

Cellular block
(see Extruded cellular fired-clay block construction)

Cement particle board
Contains particles of wood fibre (like chipboard (wood particle board)) bound together by cement. It has strength, moisture resistance, durability and thermal mass.

CLTP – Cross-laminated Timber Panels
A method of construction originating from mainland Europe, which makes use of forest thinnings of small diameter. It usually consists of same-sized square battens bonded to create a sheet one batten thick. To this is added two or more layers of the same, but each layer is arranged at right angles to the previous layer, and all are adhered to each other. This makes a very strong, dimensionally stable, rigid panel from which structural panels are cut to size and shape.

Code for Sustainable Homes
An environmental assessment method for rating and certifying the performance of new homes. It is a national standard for use in the design and construction of new homes with a view to encouraging continuous improvement in sustainable home building, and reduced carbon in use.

Ecological assessment
A comprehensive assessment of the likely ecological impacts of proposed developments on a site. This can take place on any type or size of site.

Ecology survey
A survey providing baseline information about the ecological characteristics of a site, including the presence or potential for protected species and their habitats.

External weather envelope
Consists of roof (pitched shallow or flat roofs) or roof terraces and recessed balconies, external walls and doors, windows and roof lights. Occasionally there are also soffits to projecting or bridging rooms over drives and passageways, or a soffit of suspended ground floors.

EIA – Environmental Impact Assessment
For larger projects or for those in more sensitive sites where projects are likely to have a significant environmental effect, an Environmental Impact Assessment (EIA) will be a legal requirement. The relevant legislation is the Town and Country Planning (Environmental Impact Assessment) (England and Wales) Regulations 1999; Planning (Assessment of Environmental Effects) Regulations (NI) 1999 and the Environmental Impact Assessment (Scotland) Regulations 1999. An EIA covers a broad range of factors, such as the effects on soil, water, air, climate and landscape, and the effects on humans, as well as species and habitat considerations.

Embodied energy
The components of embodied energy are the manufacturing, the transportation and the disposal energy.

EPI – Environmental Performance Indicators
Environmental Performance Indicators (EPIs) are needed when evaluating the environmental performance of, for example, activities, processes, hardware and services. They are used for monitoring and benchmarking against the performance of others in the same sector, for example in SMARTWaste how many tonnes of waste per square metre of floor area of development.

Extruded cellular fired clay block construction
Extruded cellular-fired clay block is a build style that originated in mainland Europe. In the UK we have a lot of coal-fired power stations that produce a waste product called PFA (pulverised fuel ash) which is used as a cement replacement and as a primary aggregate substitute. These have been used to make lower embodied energy ingredients for high embodied energy manufacturing, steam autoclaved, aerated, concrete blocks in the UK. (In mainland Europe there is a predominance of nuclear and hydro-electric power stations, so concrete blocks are not a normal part of their industry.) These cellular-fired clay blocks are extruded, creating lots of air cells that trap air and create long path routes through the block for conducted heat, so offering a good U value. The blocks also have a thermal mass and moisture mass, helping to moderate both the temperature and humidity of the spaces adjacent to the blocks.

Forest thinnings
Ideally, this term should be 'plantation thinnings' in order to be accurate. Tree plantations are created by the close planting of saplings to encourage competitive and straight growth. As the trees grow they become too crowded, so alternate rows of trees are removed; this can happen a few times over the lifecycle of the crop in the plantation. As the process is repeated, the removed trees are progressively bigger and can yield useful timber, but the sections may be small and restrict the timber applications, so materials and methods of construction have been invented to exploit these arisings and avoid them becoming waste or just biomass fuel. CLTPs are a good example.

Habitat
The area or environment where an organism or ecological community normally lives or occurs.

Habitat creation
The establishment of a new habitat, often required as compensation for development and loss of an ecosystem. Can include bat box installations and pond creations.

Low carbon

Low carbon buildings (LCB) are buildings which are specifically engineered with carbon dioxide reduction in mind. So by definition an LCB is a building which emits significantly less carbon dioxide than regular buildings. There is at the moment no emissions threshold under which a building would qualify as an LCB. But to be genuinely carbon (climate change) neutral, an LCB would have to achieve at least 80% carbon reduction compared with regular buildings.

Luminaire

Light fitting or unit designed to distribute light from a lamp.

Mitigation

Where adverse effects are unavoidable, measures are taken to minimise negative impacts. This is not the subject of this book.

Moisture mass

Materials with moisture-absorbent properties, for example unfired clay, can be used as a plaster skim or finish on walls and ceilings. If there is a sufficient amount of the material and when the air is saturated, the clay can absorb moisture from the atmosphere and hold it in the body of the material until conditions improve, then release the moisture again. Walls with absorbent surfaces are said to have moisture mass. For people who live in 'fuel poverty' and who cannot afford to heat their properties or who choose paraffin heating that generates high levels of moisture in the air, the risks of surface moulds are high and moisture mass is a property that will be beneficial. However, impermeable paints applied to them will prevent this function from occurring.

Nest boxes

A man-made box in which animals, such as birds, can nest. These are aimed at replacing or supplementing natural nest sites, such as farm buildings and old houses. Specialist nest boxes are available for different bird species.

Non-toxic

Toxic treatments, paints or stains are very harmful to wildlife. Bats and birds can be poisoned by toxic timber treatment, so wood should be either left untreated or treated using non-toxic options. There is a growing market in non-toxic wood treatments which are made from natural ingredients and are environmentally friendly.

Non-toxic boards

Boards used in boxes for birds and bats need to be durable, but this should not be achieved by preservative treatment or paints or stains, all of which could be harmful to wildlife.

Parge coat

A single base coat of plaster applied to the inside face of masonry walls to achieve a level of air-tightness before applying plasterboard drylining. Ironically, plasterboard was introduced to eliminate wet trade plaster, and parge coats reintroduce them.

Passive solar orientation

Orientating towards or facing the sun, and positioning rooms on the correct side of the building to gain the heat. Overshadowing by other building and trees can complicate this process.

Plywood

A timber panel product made of many thin leaves of wood glued together with grain direction arranged at right angles to provide strength in both directions. Adhesives and preservative treatment can make them durable, but also toxic. Durable species can be chosen, but care must be taken to avoid unsustainable clear felling and illegal logging. Chain of Custody (awarded to companies who can demonstrate that their products contain wood from well-managed forests) and plantation certification help to avoid this. To summarise, the key points are:

- Avoid tropical species unless FSC (Forest Stewardship Council) certified or exhibiting the FSC Label.
- INT – internal grade plywood.
- Water and Boil Proof (WBP) plywood are suitable for external and humid, damp conditions.
- Shuttering plywood is suitable for internal barn owl boxes.
- Tea chests using plywood are suitable for reuse as barn owl boxes. Smooth any sharp edges.
- Marine Grade Plywood is suitable for boat building (excessive in most construction applications).
- Always look for the BSI Kitemark and get what you are paying extra for.

PV – Photovoltaic cells

A module incorporating a semiconductor that generates electricity when exposed to daylight or sunlight.

SIPs – Structural insulation panel system

A panelised modern method of construction developed in mainland Europe, adopted in the UK. They use foamed insulation as a part of the structural performance of the panel, thus enabling reduced thickness of panel.

Solar gain

Direct solar radiation from the sun's rays passing through windows, roof lights and glazed areas to provide warmth to rooms and spaces. Optimal gains come from south to south-west facing glazed areas.

Solar shading shelves (brise soleil)

These are sunlight and daylight shading shelves above windows. Solar shading shelves may be adopted by birds as a nesting site at the top of a building because they will not be overlooked by windows.

Solar blinkers

These are sunlight and daylight shading blades besides windows, usually placed to the south of east or west facing windows.

Thermal mass

The ability of construction materials to absorb, store and release heat. Buildings constructed of dense materials, such as bricks or concrete, usually have a better thermal mass than lightweight buildings, such as timber, but choice of finishing materials can provide it.

Thermal store

A thermal store is a structure typically made from a material with high thermal mass. These materials are capable of absorbing and retaining heat, for example usually, but not solely, from the sun, and slowly releasing the heat back into the building when space temperature falls. In environmentally sustainable building, thermal stores are used as a passive means of maintaining a constant internal space temperature, therefore reducing the need for mechanical heating and cooling. These stores are often designed to be part of the internal fabric of the building, usually in the form of a high density wall or floor situated near a heat source. Materials with high thermal mass include masonry, rock and water.

Timber frame

Timber frame as we know it is not timber post and beam construction used in traditional building construction. Today the term is used to describe timber stud framework, usually panellised (sometimes known as cassette panels), which may or may not be pre-insulated. They are usually available as kits or to bespoke designs.

U value

This is a measure of thermal transmittance through the fabric of a building. U values give a measure of air-to-heat transmission (loss or gain) due to the thermal conductance of the material, for example from inside to outside a building. The lower the U value, the lower the building fabric's thermal conductance (k-value) and the better the material performs thermally. Approved Document L to the Building Regulations and the Code for Sustainable Homes dictate the maximum U value of elements of buildings; designers can improve on these.

U value envelope

This refers to all the parts of the external envelope of the building that keep the heat in and the cold out. It consists of the roof (pitched shallow or flat roofs) or roof terraces and recessed balconies, external walls, ground/basement floor (suspended or ground bearing), and doors, windows and roof lights. Occasionally there are also soffits to projecting or bridging rooms over drives and passageways, or a soffit of suspended ground floors. Each part will contain structure, thermal insulation, weather or rising damp barriers, wind tight and airtight barriers or vapour barriers, and breather membranes to make sure the insulation works well and for the life of the building without gaining moisture which may affect its performance. Occasionally the U value envelope is not the external weather envelope, for example the flat ceiling below a pitched roof – in this case the insulation is at ceiling level and the attic is allowed to be cold in winter and hot in summer. If there is a water storage cistern in the attic, the U value envelope needs the ceiling insulation to wrap up and over the cistern. Walls between the house and integral garages also have lesser requirements to external walls. Since the garage door is less likely to have a good U value, this wall should be the U value envelope and be the same as an external wall U value.

Unimproved grassland

This is permanent grassland that has either never been subject to agricultural improvement or where that improvement was insignificant and the effects have now disappeared.

Wildlife conservation

The protection, preservation, management or restoration of species and their habitats. Efforts are aimed at preventing the depletion of present populations and ensuring the continued existence of the habitats that targeted species need to survive.

Wildlife garden

A wildlife garden is an environment that is attractive to a range of wildlife, including birds, amphibians, reptiles, insects and mammals. A wildlife garden will usually contain a variety of habitats that have either been deliberately created by the gardener or have been allowed to establish by minimising maintenance and intervention, avoiding the use of any damaging pesticides.

Wood preservatives

Wood preservative are generally designed to kill living organisms like spores and fungus that might try to consume the nutritional parts of the timber and, consequently, are toxic to other living forms. Natural England maintain a list of chemicals wood preservatives that are safe for use in bat roosts if applied as instructed and when the bats are not present.

Wood preservatives excluded

Choosing durable species of timber, usually hardwood, but not exclusively, means timber can be used in numerous situations with different exposure levels without preservative treatment and will last longer.

Zero carbon

Since the publication of the Government's plans to achieve zero carbon in all new homes from 2016, and in all new non-domestic buildings from 2019, there have been calls from the industry for a clear definition of 'zero carbon'. The basic definition is that a zero carbon home is one whose net carbon dioxide emissions, taking account of emissions associated with all energy use in the home, is equal to zero or negative across the year, as outlined by the Minister of State, John Healey MP, in August 2009.

References

Commission for Architecture and the Built Environment (CABE) (2005a) *Does Money Grow on Trees?* London: CABE.

Commission for Architecture and the Built Environment (CABE) (2005b) *Start with the Park. Creating Sustainable Urban Green Spaces in Areas of Housing Growth.* London: CABE.

Commission for Architecture and the Built Environment (CABE) (2006) *Making Contracts Work for Wildlife. How to Encourage Biodiversity in Parks.* London: CABE.

Commission for Architecture and the Built Environment (CABE) (2007) *It's Our Space. A Guide for Community Groups Working to Improve Public Spaces.* London: CABE.

Commission for Architecture and the Built Environment (CABE) (2008) *Building for Life.* London: CABE.

Department for Business, Enterprise and Regulatory Reform (BERR) (2008) *Strategy for Sustainable Construction.* HM Government in association with the Strategic Forum for Construction. London: BERR.

Department for Environment, Food and Rural Affairs (Defra) (2006) *The UK Biodiversity Action Plan: Highlights from the 2005 reporting round.* London: Defra. Published on behalf of the UK Biodiversity Partnership.

Department for Environment, Food and Rural Affairs (Defra) (2007) *Guidance for Local Authorities on Implementing the Biodiversity Duty* London: Defra.

Department for Environment, Food and Rural Affairs (Defra) (2008a) *Populations of Wild Birds in England.* England Biodiversity Strategy Indicators (Part H1(a)). London: Defra.

Department for Environment, Food and Rural Affairs (Defra) (2008b) *Populations of Butterflies in England.* England Biodiversity Strategy Indicators (Part H1(b)). London: Defra.

Drewitt, E. J. A and Dixon, N. (2008) Diet and Prey Selection of Urban Dwelling Peregrine Falcons in Southwest England. *British Birds*, 101, pp. 58–67.

European Communities (EC) (2008) *The Economics of Ecosystems and Biodiversity.* Brussels: Commission of the European Communities. Available at http://ec.europa.eu.

Handley, J., Pauleit, S., Slinn, P., Barber, A., Baker, M., Jones, C. and Lindley, S. (2003) *Accessible Natural Green Space Standards in Towns and Cities: A Review and Toolkit for their Implementation.* English Nature Research Reports Number 526. Peterborough: English Nature.

Horwitz, P., Lindsay, M. and O'Connor, M. (2001) Biodiversity, Endemism, Sense of Place and Public Health: Inter-relationships for Australian Inland Aquatic Systems. *Ecosystem Health*, 7, pp. 253–265.

Margerison, C. (2008) *A Response from the British Ecological Society and the Institute of Biology to the Environmental Audit Committee Inquiry in to 'Halting UK Biodiversity Loss'.* London: The British Ecological Society.

Morgan, C. (2006) *Design and Detailing for Airtightness. SEDA Design Guides for Scotland: No. 2* Edinburgh: Scottish Ecological Design Association (SEDA).

Mitchell-Jones, A. J. (2004) *Bat Mitigation Guidelines.* Peterborough: English Nature.

Natural Economy Northwest (2008) *The Economic Value of Green Infrastructure.* Natural Economy Northwest. Available at www.naturaleconomynorthwest.co.uk/resources+reports.php.

Natural England (2009) *No Charge? Valuing the Natural Environment.* Sheffield: Natural England.

Office of the Deputy Prime Minister (2005a) *Biodiversity and Geological Conservation – Statutory Obligations and their Impact within the Planning System.* Government Circular 06/2005. London: HMSO.

Office of the Deputy Prime Minister (2005b) *Planning Policy Statement 9: Biodiversity and Geological Conservation.* London: HMSO.

Office of the Deputy Prime Minister (2006) *Planning for Biodiversity and Geological Conservation: A Guide to Good Practice.* London: HMSO.

Planning Service (1997) *Planning Policy Statement 2: Planning and Nature Conservation.* Belfast: The Planning Service.

Pollard, A. (2009) *Visual Constraints on Bird Behaviour.* University of Cardiff.

Ramsden, D. and Twiggs, M. (2009). *Barn Owls and Rural Planning Applications .What needs to happen – A Guide for Planners.* Barn Owl Trust: Ashburton.

Rodríguez, A., García, A. M., Cervera, F. and Palacios, V. (2006) Landscape and anti-predation determinants of nest-site selection, nest distribution and productivity in a Mediterranean population of Long-eared Owls, *Asio otus. Ibis*, 148(1), pp. 133–145.

Schofield, H. W. (2008) *The Lesser Horseshoe Bat Conservation Handbook.* Ledbury: The Vincent Wildlife Trust.

Scottish Government (1999) *National Planning Policy Guide 14: Natural Heritage.* Edinburgh: Scottish Government.

Scottish Government (2000) *Planning Advice Note 60: Planning for Natural Heritage.* Edinburgh: Scottish Executive Development Department.

Shawyer, C. R. (1987) *The Barn Owl in the British Isles: Its Past, Present and Future.* London: The Hawk Trust.

Stone, E. L., Jones, G. and Harris, S. (2009) Street lighting disturbs commuting bats. *Current Biology*, 19, pp. 1–5.

Town and Country Planning Association (2009) *Biodiversity positive: Eco-towns Biodiversity Worksheet.* London: TCPA. Available at www.tcpa.org.uk/data/files/etws_biodiversity.pdf.

Welsh Assembly Government (2009) *Technical Advice Note 5: Nature Conservation and Planning.* Cardiff: Welsh Assembly Government.

Wembridge, D. (2007) *Living with Mammals.* London: People's Trust for Endangered Species and Mammals Trust UK.

Bibliography

Arnott, S. (2007) *Wildlife on Allotments*. Peterborough: Natural England.

Balmer, D. E., Adams, S. Y. and Crick, H. Q. P. (2000) *Report on Barn Owl Release Scheme: Monitoring Project Phase II*. BTO Research Report No. 250. Available at www.defra.gov.uk.

Bat Conservation Trust (2006) *A Review of the Success of Bat Boxes in Houses*. Scottish Natural Heritage, Commissioned Report No. 160. Inverness: Scottish Natural Heritage.

Dixon, N. and Shawyer, C. (2005) *Peregrine Falcons – Provision of Artificial Nest Sites on Built Structures. Advice Note for Conservation Organisations, Local Authorities and Developers*. London: London Biodiversity Partnership. Available at www.lbp.org.uk/downloads/ Publications/Management/peregrine_nest-box_advice.pdf.

Early, P., Gedge, D., Newton, J. and Wilson, S. (2007) *Building Greener. Guidance on the Use of Green Roofs, Green Walls and Complementary Features on Buildings*. London: CIRIA.

Fox, R., Conrad, K. F., Parsons, M. S., Warren, M. S. and Woiwod, I. P. (2000) *The State of Britain's Larger Moths*. Wareham, Dorset: Butterfly Conservation and Rothamsted Research.

Gedge, D., Dunnet, N., Grant, G. and Jones, R. (2007) *Living Roofs*. Peterborough: Natural England.

HM Government (2009) *Strategy for Sustainable Construction Progress Report*. Crown copyright.

Ketchin, M. of Simpson and Brown Architects (1998) *The Design and Construction of Bat Boxes in Houses – A Guide to the Installation of Roost Boxes for Bats in Existing Scottish Houses*. Perth: Scottish Natural Heritage.

Mitchell-Jones, A. J. and McLeish, A. P. (2004) *Bat Workers' Manual*, 3rd edn. Peterborough: JNCC.

National Trust and English Heritage (2010) *Wildlife and Buildings*. Forthcoming publication by the National Trust and English Heritage.

Oxford, M. (2001) *Developing Naturally: A Handbook for Incorporating the Natural Environment into Planning and Development*. London: Association of Local Government Ecologists.

Rich, C. and Longcore, T. (eds) (2006) *Ecological Consequences of Artificial Night Lighting*. Washington: Island Press.

Royal Commission on Environmental Pollution (2009) *Artificial Light in the Environment*. London: HMSO.

Royal Society for the Protection of Birds (RSPB) (2002) *Unravelling the Web: The Global Value of Wild Nature*. Sandy, Bedfordshire: RSPB. Available at www.rspb.org.uk/Images/Global%20values_tcm9-133024.pdf.

Swift, S. M. (2004) *Bat Boxes: Survey of Types Available and Their Efficiency as Alternative Roosts, and Further Progress on the Development of Heated Bat Houses*. The Bat Conservation Trust and Mammals Trust UK.

UK Green Building Council (2009) *Biodiversity and the Built Environment. A Report by the UK-GBC Task Group*. London: UK Green Building Council. Available at www.ukgbc.org.

Wilby, R. L. and Perry, G. L. W. (2006) Climate change, biodiversity and the urban environment: a critical review based on London. *Progress in Physical Geography*, 30(1), pp. 73–98.

Useful websites

Conservation and wildlife
BAP
  www.bap.org.uk
Barn Owl Trust
  www.barnowltrust.org.uk
Bat Conservation Trust
  www.bats.org.uk
Biodiversity Planning Toolkit
  www.biodiversityplanningtoolkit.com
Black redstarts
  www.blackredstarts.org.uk
BBC Breathing Places
  www.bbc.co.uk/breathingplaces
British Trust for Conservation Volunteers
  www.btcv.org
British Trust for Ornithology
  www.bto.org
Buglife
  www.buglife.org.uk
Butterfly Conservation
  www.butterfly-conservation.org
Countryside Council for Wales
  www.ccw.gov.uk/?lang=en
Department for Environment, Food and Rural Affairs
  www.defra.gov.uk
Joint Nature Conservation Committee
  www.jncc.gov.uk
Living Roofs
  www.livingroofs.org
Natural England
  www.naturalengland.org.uk
Northern Ireland Environment Agency
  www.ehsni.gov.uk
People's Trust for Endangered Species
www.ptes.org
Royal Society for the Protection of Birds
  www.rspb.org.uk
Scottish Natural Heritage
  www.snh.org.uk
Swift Conservation
  www.swift-conservation.org
Vincent Wildlife Trust
  www.vwt.org.uk
Wildlife Trusts
  www.wildlifetrusts.org

Ecologists
Association of Local Government Ecologists
  www.alge.org.uk
Association of Wildlife Trust Consultancies
  www.awtc.co.uk
Institute of Ecology and Environmental Management
  www.ieem.net
Institute of Environmental Management and Assessment
  www.iema.net

Planning
Biodiversity Planning Toolkit
  www.biodiversityplanningtoolkit.com
Department for Communities and Local Government
  www.communities.gov.uk
Northern Ireland Environment Agency
  www.ehsni.gov.uk
Planning Portal
  www.planningportal.gov.uk
Royal Town Planning Institute
  www.rtpi.org.uk
Scottish Government
  www.scotland.gov.uk
Town and Country Planning Association
  www.tcpa.org.uk
Welsh Assembly Government
  http://new.wales.gov.uk

Industry
Chartered Institute of Building
  www.ciob.org.uk
Commission for Architecture and the Built Environment
  www.cabe.org.uk
Department for Business, Innovation and Skills
  www.bis.gov.uk
GreenSpec
  www.greenspec.co.uk
Institution of Lighting Engineers
  www.ile.org.uk
Royal Institute of British Architects
  www.architecture.com
Royal Institution of Chartered Surveyors
  www.rics.org
UK Green Building Council
  www.ukgbc.org

Products
Forticrete
  www.forticrete.co.uk
Ibstock
  www.ibstock.com
Norfolk Bat Brick
  www.norfolk-bat-group.org.uk
RoofBLOCK
  www.roofblock.co.uk
Schwegler
  www.schwegler-nature.com
Tudor Roof Tiles
  www.tudorrooftiles.co.uk

Index

Image credits

Cover images: (front) CG image of housing, courtesy of zedfactory.com
(back) Steve Parker/Bat Conservation Trust

Page

ii	R. J. Brookes/Bat Conservation Trust
viii	Hugh Clark/Bat Conservation Trust
x	Kevin Keatley/Barn Owl Trust
xiv	Hugh Clark/Bat Conservation Trust
3	(top) Steven Roe/Bat Conservation Trust
	(bottom) John Haddow/Bat Conservation Trust
4	Gareth Jones/Bat Conservation Trust
5	Amir Ben Dov, Israel, courtesy of Swift Conservation
7	Tommy Holden/British Trust for Ornithology
8	(top) John Harding/British Trust for Ornithology
	(bottom) Allan Drewitt/Natural England
9	Allan Drewitt/Natural England
10	David Ramsden/Barn Owl Trust
11	Jon Salloway
12	Amir Ben Dov, Israel
22	Nick Sampford/Barn Owl Trust
30	Tudor Roof Tile Co. Limited
31	Ibstock Brick Ltd
32	RoofBLOCK Ltd
33	Ibstock Brick Ltd
34	Forticrete Ltd
35	John Goldsmith/Bat Conservation Trust
36	Schwegler GmbH
37	Schwegler GmbH
42	Ibstock Brick Ltd
43	Schwegler GmbH
44	Schwegler GmbH
45	Schwegler GmbH
46	Schwegler GmbH
47	Schwegler GmbH
49	Schwegler GmbH
50	Schwegler GmbH
51	RoofBLOCK Ltd
54	David Ramsden/Barn Owl Trust
55	David Ramsden/Barn Owl Trust
84	Bere Architects
85	(top) Livingroofs.org
	(bottom) AECOM Design + Planning
88	Kevin Durose/Bat Conservation Trust
90	(top) Russell Westwood/Natural England
	(bottom) Alex Pollard
91	Hugh Clark/Bat Conservation Trust
92	Emma Stone
94	Peter Wakely/Natural England
96	Anne Youngman/Bat Conservation Trust
97	Peter Wakely/Natural England